ALLY LE

HOW TO LEAD PEOPLE WHO ARE NOT LIKE YOU

STEPHANIE CHUNG

Ally Leadership: How to Lead People Who Are Not Like You

Copyright ©2024 Stephanie Chung

CHUNG, STEPHANIE Author
ALLY LEADERSHIP
STEPHANIE CHUNG

Published by:
ELITE ONLINE PUBLISHING
63 East 11400 South
Suite #230
Sandy, UT 84070
EliteOnlinePublishing.com

ISBN: 978-1-961801-43-1 (Hardcover)
ISBN: 978-1-961801-44-8 (Paperback)
ISBN: 978-1-961801-45-5 (eBook)
ISBN: 978-1-961801-46-2 (Audiobook)

Editing and publishing support provided by The Write Image Consulting, LLC and Write Your Life.

BUS071000
BUS118000
BUS019000

QUANTITY PURCHASES: Schools, companies, professional groups, clubs, and other organizations may qualify for special terms when ordering quantities of this title. For information, email info@eliteonlinepublishing.com.

Are you an Ally Leader?

Take the Ally Leadership Assessment to find out.

StephanieChung.com/bonus

It's okay to not be perfect at "allyship." We all need help. With this book you'll get the guidance you need to show up as a true Ally Leader in every aspect of your life.

PRAISE FOR
STEPHANIE CHUNG

The truth is, I would read just about anything Stephanie Chung wrote. Any subject, proven expertise or not. But to have a book that distills her well-lived and hard-earned insights on leadership is a privilege, a pleasure, and an actionable advantage. Her passion for humanity and excellence has charted a path worth following. As usual, Stephanie safeguards nothing, sharing freely the proven formula for collective success she has used and learned along the way.

Clint Bruce
Founder of TRG, HoldFast, and the HighGround Foundation
Naval Academy Graduate, Former Naval Special Warfare Officer

The professional bookshelf has long needed a warm welcome from a C-suite black woman to would-be allies of all backgrounds on how to practice less shame and more leadership. This book by Stephanie Chung, a history-making aviation executive, does just that. Her candid writing on privilege shares entirely new language that every American should read.

Lisa Stone
Co-founder, BlogHer, BrainTrust Founders Studio

Ally Leadership is a masterclass in navigating today's diverse workforce. It's the essential guide for any leader aiming to inspire, connect, and thrive in a world where differences are the norm and inclusivity is the path to success.

Michael Port
WSJ bestselling author of *Steal the Show*

As a combat-proven military leader with extensive experience leading individuals from all walks of life, I am deeply impressed by Stephanie Chung's *Ally Leadership: How To Lead People Who Are Not Like You*. This book is a vital resource for any leader striving to navigate the complexities of our diverse modern workforce.

Jason Harris
Lt. Col., US Air Force (Retired)
Keynote Speaker and Senior Leadership Advisor

Ally Leadership: How to Lead People Who Are Not Like You is the must-have playbook for any leader in today's diverse and ever-evolving workforce. Stephanie offers leaders practical advice on supporting their teams while still maintaining business goals. A perfect read for those who aspire to be in leadership roles and an essential read for those already in them.

Bozoma Saint John
Hall of Fame Marketer, author of *The Urgent Life*,
and *Entrepreneur*

This book is a game-changer for leadership; a must read for experienced, new, and aspiring leaders! It is a refreshing and powerful exploration of personal learning and awareness, allyship, and inclusion as the keys to winning in business (and in life). Stephanie Chung has mastered the art of storytelling to demonstrate how to navigate complex situations by taking action in a way that allows everyone to win. Absolutely brilliant!

Kimberly Evans
EVP, Corporate Head of Sustainability, Inclusion,
& Social Impact, Northern Trust

What I appreciated most about this book is the stories filled with practical advice and next steps. She addresses and acknowledges the fact that hard topics exist in the workplace. At the same time, she doesn't take sides on the topics. Instead, she tells us that we have a choice in how we deal with people who have differing viewpoints and are different from us.

David Ashcraft
President and CEO, Global Leadership Network

This is a critical read for anyone in leadership, thinking about leadership, or wanting better leadership. Chung dives into specific strategies that will transform the way you engage the important people on your team.

Vanessa Van Edwards
Bestselling Author and Founder of Science of People

To my entire family, especially my mom and dad,
my husband, Sam, and my daughter, Brittany.
I love you all.
Thank you for always making me smile!

TABLE OF CONTENTS

FOREWORD

YOU HAVE THIS BOOK IN your hands because you want better. To be better, to help others be better. You're down with what psychologist and author Carol Dweck called the "growth mindset"—the idea that a person's ability in any domain is not fixed but can develop through effort.

So, let's get straight to the point: Ally Leadership is what it's really about. From the Latin alligare meaning to bind together. Cue the *High School Musical* earworm, "We're All In This Together," per my fifteen years at Disney. Guiding each other safely on their journey, but from a connective place. A partnership of peers. Empathy.

When I learned sympathy means feeling *for* and empathy means feeling *with*, my mind was blown. I started to change how I connected *with* individuals, especially in challenging times. The difference between the two concepts implores one to not think about titles or levels, or superiors versus subordinates. Empathy is finding the common while respecting the uncommon. We're talking Golden Rule stuff here. As Dutch consultant Alexander den Heijer notes, "When I talk to managers I get the feeling they're important. When I talk to leaders I get the feeling I'm important."

Let me tell you why I love this book and why you are likely to want to buy more copies for others.

You'll learn to start at Privilege Awareness—a great empathy exercise and the baseline for any personal growth. You'll learn to "navigate the narrows." And you will never forget ALLY as the Ask-Listen-Learn-You acronym.

Ally Leadership is about everyone, so this book is, therefore, for everyone. For years, my management mindset was exclusive and exclusionary, as I thought leaders were only found among extroverts. I thought leaders got where they did with skilled oration. Turns out introverts are as essential in leadership. Turns out listening matters as much as speaking.

I have always been "male and pale." And now too, more recently, "stale and frail." Ally Leadership is an instructional manual for businessfolks like me trying to navigate the New New, a "Relevance for Dummies" book.

Words matter, and this wildly well-written collection of them will get you thinking about how words are used and received. For us professional brand marketers, nomenclature has done a 180 over the last century, from referencing Us (our company's identity, values, differentiation) to referencing You (your benefit, your experience, your improved need-states). We have gone from chest-beating ("everyday low prices," "king of beers," etc.) to ears-wide-open (UberEats' "Tonight I'll be having," Peloton's "We all have our reasons") as the power has shifted—supercharged by technology—from Brand to Consumer.

So too should your words as a Leader do a 180. Going from I to we, from what needs getting done to who needs being served.

But do not get triggered. While ideals like Diversity and Equity and Inclusion are implicit to seeking understanding, this book is much bigger than categorizations and this Ally Leadership movement is timeless rather than trendy.

Stephanie Chung is an extraordinary businessperson and human. Baseball scouts call people like her the "five tool player," that "oh so rare" individual who can hit for power, hit for average, run, throw, and field. Stephanie Chung is a five-tool friggin' All-Star in global business—Salesperson, Leader, Speaker, Consultant, and now Author. All of that slathered in a gravy (ew) of Kindness.

I ain't much for book learnin', but trust, you are about to embark on a journey that entertains, challenges, instructs, and inspires. Ally Leadership is a movement, and you and I are in this movement together. With every page you read, with every thought you reconsider, with every executive action you revise from now forward.

Thank you for your consideration, fellow Ally.

Allyship as in Kindness. And may I close by reminding you, dear reader, that life is ultimately too damn short, and management books are too damn insignificant, for us to think about anything other than kindness.

John Rood
Chief Brand and Communications Officer, Magid
Former executive with Disney and Warner Bros.

FOREWORD

I'VE ALWAYS BELIEVED THAT THE most valuable advice comes from those who've been there and done that, which is why I connected with Stephanie Chung from the moment we met. Through a Zoom screen, she exuded a warmth that made me want to reach through the screen and give her a big hug. It was like I had known her forever, a girlfriend, a kindred spirit, a sister from another mother. Our initial encounter led to a heartfelt exchange of stories about navigating the challenges of being the "only" in various professional settings and how we've leveraged those experiences to rewrite the rules of leadership.

I always called ours "the uncorporate rules," versus the corporate "traditional" rules that made no sense. We share a conviction that the traditional rules of the workplace, crafted over a century ago by men for men, are no longer sufficient in today's world. I was tired of always being the exception to their rules and getting in trouble because those rules didn't work for me. I guess you would say that I broke the rules that made no sense and wrote the new ones. It was time to break away from outdated norms and reconstruct them to better suit our modern workforce that includes people from various backgrounds, perspectives, and skillsets. It's this rebellious spirit that earned me the moniker of Chief Troublemaker, while Stephanie channels her insights into a book titled *Ally Leadership*.

It's not that the original rules were inherently flawed; rather, they were simply out of touch with the realities of today when we have women and other historically marginalized groups in the workforce. Ending yesterday's conventions of closed-door deals, and embracing a new era that welcomes everyone to the table is at the heart of Stephanie's mission.

Stephanie Chung's approach to leadership is undeniably inspiring. She is reshaping workplace norms and championing "allyship" in a way that reflects a profound understanding of today's evolving workforce dynamics. Her emphasis on collaboration, empathy, and genuine care for all individuals resonates deeply, particularly in an era where team alignment and cooperation are paramount for effective leadership. Her strategic vision and empathy-driven leadership style set a powerful example for aspiring leaders.

What I particularly admire about Stephanie is her choice of terminology—she refers to "ally leaders" instead of "male allies." This distinction is crucial because when we use the term "male allies," it inherently assumes that men hold the power. However, by embracing the term "ally leaders," Stephanie neutralizes the language, suggesting that any leader in a position of authority should leverage their power for positive change. It's a powerful reminder that language matters in shaping perceptions and driving measurable success. The principles outlined in *Ally Leadership* are not mere theoretical concepts; they are practical strategies grounded in real-world experience.

Stephanie's journey from humble beginnings to becoming the first African American woman to lead a private aviation company is a testament to her resilience and innovation. She brings a wealth of experience in leading diverse teams, coupled with a deep commitment to fostering inclusive workplaces where every voice is heard and valued. Her book, *Ally Leadership*, serves as a playbook for creating environments where everyone can thrive and find fulfillment in their work. Drawing from her own experiences and insights, Stephanie offers practical guidance for leaders who are committed to driving positive change and championing wins for their teams.

As we embark on this journey towards a more expansive and empathetic future of leadership, Stephanie's voice serves as a guiding light. Her unwavering dedication to seeing everyone win, coupled with her genuine leadership style, sets a powerful example for leaders everywhere. With Stephanie's principles as our compass, we can navigate the complexities of today's workforce with clarity, compassion, and purpose.

Shelley Zalis
Founder and CEO, The Female Quotient

INTRODUCTION

THE LEADER OF THE 21ST century needs to know how to effectively lead every race, creed, gender, and generation. And by "lead" them, I don't mean dish out assignments, sign off on their quarterly reviews, and hire/fire as needed. Leading people necessitates building quality, authentic relationships with them. That requires you to know what matters to them and to seek to understand without judging.

Leading people who are not like you is not a race, religion, gender, or age issue; this is an everyone issue. We all need help with Ally Leadership. No one gets everyone. The need for Ally Leadership impacts every leader from North America to South America, from Europe to Africa, from Asia to Antarctica, and everywhere in between.

Initiatives created to tap into the skills, strengths, and intellect of all employees often lack the instructions to guide leaders in managing various viewpoints and ushering the very best of everyone into the process. White men are not solely the problem, nor is their adaptation the only solution to this ever-evolving reality. We all need to lead by example, even when we don't have all the answers or know exactly what to do.

This book is for leaders who want to stop pretending they know it all, who acknowledge that their way is not the only way, and who lean into learning as much as possible about people who are not like them. The changes happening within the workforce will cause every leader to eventually lead people who are not like them. Change is here. People who don't share your same race, religion, gender, age, social class, or sexual orientation are not going away. Burying your head in the sand won't make them disappear or conform to your standards or make it any easier to get the results you want. Ignoring the obvious signs, the intrinsic potentialities, and the inevitable results of change will only make your life and your job harder. Adopting the stance of an Ally Leader will help.

This book is for every leader who is, wants to be, or thinks they are an ally, to support you and provide you with the tools to help you become the best leader you can be. Ally Leadership is the new leadership in the 21st century, and it's a requirement of any leader who wants to remain relevant.

Ally Leadership begins with understanding that people are not all alike, which is not only okay, but is also an asset. When people are led correctly, their differences become a powerful tool for extraordinary success. In order to continue to win in leadership, all leaders need to become culturally intelligent so we can effectively connect with our team members and employees. Being culturally intelligent is about having the skills to adapt and excel in unfamiliar settings, where conversations and customs shift outside of our comfort zone.

Ally Leadership is about effectively leading people who are not like you. In the decades that I served as an executive in the high-profile aviation industry, I led many people who were not black, straight, and female like me. For you, it might be people on your team who are not white, male, and conservative, or people who are not Hispanic, Asian, gay, liberal, in the same social class, or who function with different physical or mental abilities.

People who are not like you hold opinions, insights, skills, and knowledge that matter in the workplace and in society more than you may realize. Often, they wonder how you (and people like you) got to be at the top of the food chain having little to no knowledge of the needs, interests, and talents of everyone else. In most instances, you are likely intimidated by, sometimes afraid of, and completely confused about them . . . and they know it.

As the world evolves, knowing how to lead people who are not like you will become more and more essential. New times call for new leadership. Gone are the days when you could lead like the leaders of the past, the "Do as I say, not as I do" leaders, or the leaders who hire friends, family, and those who look like them—whether they are qualified or not—in order to keep the status quo and remain within their comfort zone.

Because of the vastness of the internet, the world is now one big melting pot. Globally, "minorities" are the majority, women are half the population, and the Zoomers (Gen Z) have overtaken the Boomers in the workplace. The workforce is younger and more racially diverse, their communication styles are different, their technical skills are advanced, and their social and emotional capabilities are unique.

Now, more than ever, the world desperately needs leaders like you. Leaders who are willing to learn. Leaders committed to building significance to and through others. Leaders who know deep down that they are called to make an impact in this world beyond just the dollars and cents. Now is the time for change, because if you don't change you will get left out and left behind. There is no way to win by ignoring this reality or trying to push against it.

The future of leadership is now, and it's called Ally Leadership.

LEADERSHIP WITHIN
THE FIERY FURNACE

GOOD LORD, IT'S HOT HERE, I thought, as I walked off the plane and onto the jet bridge in Dallas, Texas. *This has to be a one-off kinda day. It can't be this hot all the time.* As I patted the sweat off of my brows, I thought, *I could never live here.*

Although I lived in Florida—another ridiculously hot and humid state—I was always amazed how differently my body reacted to the Texas weather. It was as if my body was telling me, "Do not get too comfortable here because we're not staying." Essentially, I loathed the place. I despised the fact that there was no ocean, that everything was flat, and that the greenery wasn't actually green but more like a dull brown. The place lacked vibrancy, but my company's North American headquarters were there so I needed to pop in every so often just to show my face.

As we pulled up to the hotel, I hopped out of the cab, excited to meet up with my team. We all exchanged hugs, handshakes, and high-fives, then one of my sales directors jokingly blurted out, "Steph, no one from headquarters knows we're in town, right?"

They were right. We were only in town for a day, and I thought it made more sense for us to meet at the hotel, knock out our agenda, and bypass all the unnecessary distractions that inevitably come with being at HQ. Sure enough, we had a great day and even finished early. I invited the dream team for drinks at a nearby restaurant, a nice send-off before we hopped back on our flights to go our separate ways.

As we walked to the restaurant and continued to complain about the smoldering heat, my phone rang. The caller ID indicated that it was my CEO's executive assistant. Surprised that she'd be calling me after hours, I shushed the team so there would be no background noise.

"Hello."

"Hi Stephanie, it's Debbie. Tom wants to know if you're in town?"

Busted! How did she know? It was as if her Jedi skills sensed that I was nearby.

"Umm, yes, actually, I am in town," I said, "but I'm flying out tonight."

"Tom wants to see you in his office tomorrow at 7:30 a.m.," she interjected before I could continue. "See you then."

And with that, she hung up.

Wait, what? My head was spinning. *Why am I being called into the principal's (I mean CEO's) office? How did he even know I was in town? And what the heck am I going to wear?* I hadn't packed a suitcase since I was only planning to be in town for a few hours. Silence fell on me and my entire team as our minds jumped to the worst-case scenario. Now, I really needed some wine!

I slept like I was lying in a casket that night because I couldn't afford to smear my makeup. The next morning, I put on my day-old clothes, freshened up my day-old makeup, brushed my teeth and hair with items from the hotel's grooming kit, and hopped into a cab, my mind racing. My team's performance was one of the best in the company. We were crushing it on all ends. What could this meeting be about? Clearly, he's not going to fire me; or is he? What the heck is happening?

Tom greeted me at the door as I entered the executive suite. A former football player, he was big in size and stature. The few times that I had interacted with him he was always kind to me. However, any leader whose team wasn't performing got the less kind version. Thankfully, I had never seen that side, and I was hoping today wouldn't be any different.

I took a seat and Tom got right to the point.

"Stephanie, I'm very impressed with your work. Your team is killing it!" he said. "Your revenue is up, your engagement scores are phenomenal, and I only hear good things about your leadership."

Well, that's a good start, I thought, and smiled broadly.

What he said next wiped that smile right off my face.

"I want you to move to Texas," he said, "and take over this sales team. It's a bigger team, you'll have more responsibilities, and you'll, of course, make more money."

Whoa! I did not see that coming. Tom was direct, concise, and matter of fact. I could tell this wasn't intended to be a lengthy two-way conversation. But there was no way I was interested in taking over a defunct team. Most of them were arrogant, egotistical, and couldn't sell worth a hoot. Not to mention that I was not even slightly interested in living in the "fiery furnace."

Momentarily frozen in shock, I slowly mustered up the courage to say, "Thank you so much for the opportunity, but I'll need to pass. I love my current team, I love where I live, and I'm very happy where I am."

Tom's entire temperament suddenly changed from cordial to blunt.

"Stephanie, cut the crap," he said. "I'm not asking you; I'm telling you. I need you to come to this division and fix this half-baked team. They haven't hit their number since their inception fourteen years ago.

"I need you to come here, do what you did with your current team, and fix this!" he added, pounding his index finger on his desk. "HR will work with you to find housing and they'll go over your compensation package. I'll see you in the office next month."

And just like that, Debbie politely escorted me to the door. I left, speechless, but fully aware that within thirty days I would be residing in the fiery furnace known as Dallas, Texas. Ugh!

Fast forward a month. I stood in front of the conference room, looking at my newly inherited team—my all white, all male team.

How am I going to lead them? Will they accept me? How will we get along? Are they willing to take direction from me?

As a black woman, I had come up through the ranks in an industry where no one looked like me. I was battle tested. I was determined. I was there to show these twenty sales directors that someone who looked—and probably was, in many areas—so different from them was more than qualified and capable of leading them. Undoubtedly, the majority of those in the room with their blank stares and a few glares were wondering. If you've ever tried to lead a team who had doubts about you—for whatever the reason—I'm sure you can relate.

After just one year, I answered all of their doubts and questions about my ability to lead them. During that first twelve months, the team hit its number for the first time ever. But my goal was not only to get the numbers up. That was a typical leadership goal, and the one foremost in Tom's mind.

No, my goal was to lead in a way that brought out the best in each team member, despite how different we might be, to become what I call an Ally Leader. During that transformative year, I earned the respect of the entire team, and they gained mine. I walked into that role as an excellent, but stereotypical leader. I left it as an Ally Leader.

Ally Leadership: Less Talk, More Action

Leading and working alongside people who are not like you is no longer a niche issue. Ally Leadership is a keen skill that all leaders must embody. It's about Asking, Listening, Learning, and You taking action—and action is what counts.

There is room at the top for everyone. Demographics are rapidly changing, and to be an effective leader in today's competitive workplace, you have to evolve. Today's leader needs to know how to lead all of God's children, every race, every creed, every gender. Relax—in my world, you won't get beat up, canceled, or made to feel guilty about a system you did not create. I want you to win as a leader, and I'm here to support you each step of the way.

From my 25-plus-year career as a leader in one of the most high-end, high-powered global corporate sectors—private aviation—and having worked with many leaders like you, who I respect and whose respect I earned, here's what I know about you:

- You've earned your place as a leader through hard work.
- You care about those you lead.
- You care about increasing the bottom line.
- You are constantly striving to do better in every area of leadership.
- You want to win.
- When you look in the mirror you want to be proud of yourself and your leadership.

What you might not realize is that when others win, you win. And that's what you're going to learn here.

Let's face it—it isn't getting any easier to be a great leader. Gone are the days when we could just focus on getting the job done. We now have the additional burden of trying to be all things to all people. There is no normal anymore. Everything is the "new norm." This new corporate reality is unfamiliar, often unchosen by leaders, and sometimes unwelcome. Yet, it is here.

You as a leader are expected to be knowledgeable in the areas of global issues, diversity and inclusion, climate change, sustainability, cyber security, artificial intelligence, and when to use him/her/they and them pronouns. You're expected to have an opinion on social injustice, abortion rights, mental health, and the various wars and terrorist attacks around the world. To lead male, female, black, white, brown, young, old, gay, straight, neurodiverse people, those with disabilities—every-body. All of this is in addition to developing a high-functioning workforce, delighting customers, managing boards, growing companies, and pulling a profit. It is exhausting!

Currently, there are five generations in the workforce: Silent, Baby Boomers, Gen-X, Millennials, and Gen-Z. In 2024, their ages ranged from about 78 to 19. And if things weren't tricky enough, the Alpha generation, born between 2010 – 2024, will soon enter the workforce. Beyond the generational differences, there are demographic differences as well. A large portion of the workforce is made up of women, ethnic minorities, and younger people (those under 35), while the majority of leaders are older, male, and non-ethnic.

The non-ethnic leaders are trying to wrap their heads around how to lead a more agile, diverse workforce. The diverse workforce is trying to wrap their heads around transitioning into leadership roles, navigating places that often weren't built with them in mind, and leading subordinates who haven't had leaders who looked like them. Couple this with the fact that each group wants something different; they have different perspectives, expectations, work ethics, and needs.

How is it possible to be an ally to every coworker you lead? It's complicated, but it's possible. When done authentically and consistently, great leaders become allies in the workplace. To effectively lead a group of people who are not like you, you must first meet them where they are, lead them from where they are, and capitalize on their unique gifts, talents, and viewpoints to help drive them and the business forward.

Meeting people where they are sounds simple to do, but it isn't. How do you know where someone is if you've never been where they are? What adjustments do you need to make? How do you know when you've gotten too close or gone too far? Why do you even need to make any adjustments at all? You're the leader, after all; shouldn't *they* all be adjusting to *you*? The answer is no.

Whether you're a leader in the marketplace, ministry, or the government, you have a responsibility to adjust to the needs of the workplace and the workforce. Gone are the days when you could sit at your desk, bark out orders, and expect everyone to fall in line. Your opinions and way of doing things are not the gold standard; they're just the way *you* do things. Other people have interests, approaches, opinions, ideas, and concerns that are equally as valid and important as yours are. As an Ally Leader, you need to have a curiosity and open mind to explore these. Are you prepared to do that?

Here's another truth: Like everyone else, you are replaceable. And the marketplace *will* replace you if you don't adjust to the evolving workforce you lead. That's just a fact.

Diverse teams have varying perspectives due to their differences in thoughts, mindset, communication style, and experience. All of this gives them a competitive advantage against traditional teams because they see, do, and review things differently. In fact, according to a UK-based *Cloverpop* study conducted in 2017, diverse teams make better business decisions 87% of the time. The *Great Place To Work* organization's June 2020 research found that diverse teams—people from different cultures, age groups, genders, and ethnic groups—show 11% higher revenue growth than traditional teams, i.e. people with similar backgrounds. Countless articles from *McKinsey & Company*, the *Society for Human Resources Management (SHRM)*, *Harvard Business Review*, and *Forbes*, to name a few, have advised us leaders on why diverse teams matter.

Although the positive financial impacts of having a diverse team are clear, there are some challenges to leading a diverse team. There can be communication barriers, cultural differences, and other factors that can lead to potential conflicts, if not managed correctly.

The varying thoughts and experiences that people bring to the table can seem foreign to you as a leader. You struggle to relate. According to a 2023 article titled "8 Pros and 6 Cons of Workforce Diversity in the Workplace" by Sujan Chaudhary in *MBA Note*, diverse teams have varying perspectives, which can disrupt team dynamics. Knowing how to successfully lead today's modern workforce is no easy feat. However, it is absolutely possible to do.

Unfortunately, little guidance is available on exactly how to lead those who are not like you. It's as if people assume you, as a leader, have some Jedi superpowers and you automatically know how to do this. Well, you don't and that's ok; that's why you're reading this book. But before we roll up our sleeves and dig into this new imperative for leaders, let's take a step back.

A New Tool for The Good Ol' Boys Network

The smell of fresh-cut grass was unmistakable, almost calming, as I stood on the deck overlooking the eighteenth hole at the world-renowned Pebble Beach Golf Course in California. The course had not yet opened and the stillness of the moment was breathtaking. As I stared off into the distance, the fog over the water and the crispness of the air embraced me. What a wonderful moment of absolute peace.

"Stephanie!"

I was jolted out of my state of bliss by my name being called from afar. As my eyes peered through the fog, I saw two gentlemen walking towards me—my sales director accompanied by an unknown figure. As they got closer, my sales director said, "Brad, I'd like to introduce you to my boss, the woman in charge, Stephanie Chung."

There was an awkward pause as Brad quickly looked me up and down in total judgment. It was as if he was viewing something he had never seen before. As I extended my hand to introduce myself and welcome him to our chalet, Brad blurted out four words that I'll never forget.

"You're in charge? Wow!"

Brad then proceeded to add, "You must be really, really good if you're in charge."

Shocked by his statement, and the fact that he said it out loud, I politely squeezed his hand, plastered a smile on my face, and looked him directly in the eyes.

"Yes, Brad, I'm in charge," I said, "and yes, I am really, really good."

Clearly tickled by my response, Brad gave me a big grin, matched my handshake, and replied in his southern drawl, "Well, it's a real pleasure to meet you, Stephanie Chung."

I wish I could say that Brad's initial reaction was the first time I had ever experienced *the look*, but unfortunately, it was not. Despite having twenty-plus years of experience in leadership, guiding mostly white men through some extremely challenging situations in one of the most high-ticket industries in business, I still faced questions about my ability to lead and deliver results.

The systems that were put in place to run the world and the world's economies were designed for and by men. Until 1920 in the United States, only men were allowed to vote. Women have been included in what is now considered a critical aspect of adult civic responsibility for little more than one-hundred years. During the first part of the 20th century, banks lent to men exclusively. In some countries, this is still the case. The result: societies that suffer with gender roles, the absence of skilled labor, intellect, and perspectives from half of the population, and social systems that struggle to adapt in the global evolution. These types of systems, when left unchecked, can lead to oblivion.

One of the oldest establishments in many societies is The Good Ol' Boys Network. The British coined the term "old boys network" to describe social and business connections among former students of elite male-only schools. The term has evolved to describe an informal network of men who share similar backgrounds and who help each other in personal and professional matters. The term also is the basis for the saying, "It's not *what* you know but *who* you know." Now, that network is being challenged and dismantled. And it's leaving a lot of leaders unsure how to proceed.

The future's biggest pivot of power will involve the dismantling of patriarchies. Patriarchy, derived from the Greek word patriarkhēs, literally means "the rule of the father." It is a system of society or government in which men control the economic, political, and religious power. Keep in mind, patriarchy is a social structure, not necessarily a conspiracy among men, meaning it's not always intentional.

The interesting thing about my interaction with Brad and others like him was that deep down inside Brad thought he was giving me a compliment. Brad wasn't trying to be *that guy*, the guy who is tone deaf and unaware of his own bias. Instead, Brad thought his backhanded compliment of me being "really, really good" would be well received by me.

Don't get me wrong, the Brads of the world are typically good guys. They're smart, kind, and friendly. They're leaders. They're people who like to win and, by all accounts, they consider themselves allies. If asked, they would insist that they are a staunch supporter of people who are not like them. The problem is that if you asked them to name three things they did that week to show their Ally Leadership, they'd be hard pressed to do so. In a time when people's BS monitors are on high alert, the Brads of the world are being canceled before they can even get out of the gate.

In the United States, much of the conversation around being an ally has centered around white men not knowing how to lead women and people of color. The conversation has operated under the premise that white men, who control a majority of the leadership positions within corporate America, simply "don't get it." To make matters worse, the conversation goes, if you're a white man, societal norms have suggested that you represent the epitome of a "normal" human being, which means that everyone else is considered an "other."

As a result, white men are finding themselves on the outskirts of programs designed for 21st-century advancement, which often focus on women, non-white employees, and those with different physical abilities.

But it's not just white men who face the unique challenges of intersectionality, i.e. spaces where different races, genders, and classes intersect. These new leaders can also find themselves struggling to lead people who are different from them, not to mention struggling to adapt to a system still dealing with the after-effects of the Good Ol' Boys Network.

No matter what you bring to the leadership table, all of us must confront, and then change, the thinking that hinders our ability to most effectively work with and lead others.

Your Mental Comfort Zone: Familiarity

What happens in your brain when you are dealing with the unfamiliar? The unfamiliar person in the workplace—you know, the one who speaks with an accent, or the one you're convinced is on the spectrum. What about the one who questions long-held corporate policies, or whose hair is different from most? These folks can cause you and others fear. But is that fear justified or is it a survival mechanism designed to keep the status quo?

It is human nature to prefer to surround ourselves with people who look like us. Check out most offices, college campuses, or churches and you will find this to be true. We often prefer the familiarity of sameness. It takes less effort and uses fewer cognitive resources to be around people who are like us.

To be around people who are not like you requires that you exert energy trying to understand their way of life. Some of this dates back to human survival as a species. Human ancestors were tribal. They communicated similarly, they looked the same, they held the same beliefs, and they ate the same foods. There was safety and comfort in familiarity.

In a 2001 study by the Department of Psychology at Stanford University titled, "Mere Exposure: A Gateway to the Subliminal," Professor and Psychologist R.B. Zajonc found that being exposed to the familiar reduces uncertainty and allows us to process information faster. This might show up in the workplace when you choose team members for a project because you think everyone will agree easily and reach consensus faster and easier. But faster isn't always best; sometimes it's just . . . fast.

Preferring the familiar is often expressed through hiring people who you believe will fit in with everyone, either because they are of the same background, ethnicity, gender, or socioeconomic status. Maybe it's promoting people who you feel most comfortable with because they're familiar and you know what to expect. Staying in your comfort zone often means going to lunch with the folks who look like you, think like you, and who you've worked with for a long time.

But being comfortable is actually a detriment because it can put you and the team at a disadvantage due to the lack of differing opinions and insights. The lack of different opinions and insights is our greatest modern threat, but our brains haven't caught up yet. Our brains are still hardwired to look for the familiar and to respond with fear when dealing with the unfamiliar. Fear causes the "fight or flight" reaction in our brain to light up like a birthday cake. This internal gut check of a reaction only strengthens when validated by action. Meaning, if you perceive that unfamiliar person to be a threat or to have mistreated you, your fear of them becomes rational in your mind.

Fear activates the amygdala, the small almond-shaped portion of your brain that is part of your brain's limbic system, the oldest part of the brain where instincts and behavioral and emotional responses are. This powerhouse controls your fear emotion, a necessary response for your overall survival.

In an April 2023 report titled, "Amygdala: What It is and What It Controls," The Cleveland Clinic notes that the amygdala processes things you see or hear and uses that input to learn what is dangerous. Your amygdala has the unique ability to skip processing steps related to your senses in order to reach safety faster. For example, if you hear a familiar sound that you deem as dangerous—like a car backfiring or a balloon popping—your amygdala immediately sends emergency signals to your brain that cause you to react before other areas of the brain can even process what the sound was. That sound causes you to jump, flinch, or crouch because your brain equates that sound with potential danger.

On the positive side, this instinctive response helped our ancestors, and now us, stay alive. The second you sense danger, your body responds. The problem is that, because it is the oldest part of your brain, the amygdala is hardwired with elements that may not always serve you well today. Think about it: to have your brain respond to someone who doesn't look like you, with the same fear your brain would create if a bear were chasing you, would not be good. Essentially, if you perceive someone different from you as a threat, with no other evidence showing they are, you would likely behave irrationally. And being irrational is not what great leaders are made of.

As an Ally Leader tasked with leading people who are not like you, controlling the signals received by the amygdala is essential. When you do not control those signals, you may jump to inaccurate conclusions about people. You may think that someone is subpar because they don't communicate their findings in the way in which you're accustomed. Or you may inadvertently play people out of position because you don't perceive them to be qualified, not based on facts but instead based on judgments driven by your unfamiliarity.

The amygdala contributes to other things as well, not just fear. In a 2021 article on *Verywell Health* titled, "The science of emotions: How the brain shapes how you feel," writer Peter Pressman states: "The amygdala also plays a role in modulating social cognition and behavior (i.e. recognizing emotions in faces, judging trustworthiness, and generating a sense of personal space). Furthermore, [you] assign positive and negative meaning to moments, converting them into what [you] recognize as happy or traumatic memories. This function helps you learn from past experiences and influences future decisions."

Consider how you "size up" your coworkers or acquaintances in social circles. Think about the person in your company or church who speaks with a deep southern drawl. You might question their competence. Or the single mom who always looks disheveled, like she's hanging on by a thread, so you question her time management skills. Or the person who struggles with their weight, so you question their self-discipline, or the introvert who you believe is antisocial. What about the guy with the tattoos, or the girl with the pink hair? You would never place them in a customer-facing position because what would customers think?

What about the way Brad sized me up at the Pebble Beach golf course? Brad eyeballed me up, down, and sideways, clearly signifying that he had never seen someone like me in that position, therefore, questioning my qualifications. The truth was that he hadn't seen anyone like me in that position before because there were no other people of color, during that time, leading at that level within the private jet industry. However, just because there wasn't anyone like me leading at that time doesn't mean that I wasn't qualified to be there, nor did it mean that there weren't others who looked like me who were also qualified to be there.

Can you think of a time when you were sized up, down and sideways, and could feel you were being judged differently? If you cannot, count yourself lucky, or consider the possibility that you have never (or very infrequently) been amid a group of people not like you. If you can recall such an experience, think about how you felt being sized up in that way. Did you feel empowered or denigrated? Supported or sidelined? Inspired or ignored? As an Ally Leader, you would never want your employees to feel that their competence was being questioned by you simply because they don't look like everyone else.

For leaders with high-performing teams in a workplace that requires teamwork and efficiency, leading through a lens of bias and fear threatens the very fabric of your existence and the outcomes of your efforts. As an Ally Leader, it's important to look introspectively to acknowledge your feelings towards people who are not like you. What beliefs do you hold that could hold you back? We all have something. As I mentioned, no one gets everyone.

KEY TAKEAWAYS

- Every leader will lead someone who is not like them.
- People not like you hold opinions, insights, and skills that matter in the workplace.

TAKE ACTION

This week, observe each meeting that you're in and ask yourself the following:

- Is there diversity of race, gender, and input in the meeting?
- Do the diverse attendees speak up in the meeting?
- When they share their thoughts, how do you and others respond?
- After a week of observations, decide what needs to be done to ensure differing voices and opinions are welcomed.

YOUR IN-GROUP SHOULD
BE A WINDOW, NOT A MIRROR

A S YOU DISCOVER THE WORLD of differences around you—in your community and within your workplace—be aware that other people's differences are not a problem for them, and they shouldn't be for you either. People are who they are. That's it. You will like some and you won't like others.

As humans, our brains tend to unconsciously place people in groups. You place people in an in-group category—"those like me" or "us"—or an out-group category—"those unlike me" or "them." The in-group typically includes people who have similar interests as you and who belong to the same political party, socioeconomic class, religion, gender, culture, or ethnicity. You identify them as being part of your social safe space. This process of categorizing people, which is natural and instinctive, takes nanoseconds and happens simply by looking at someone. It is also unfair, limiting, and rooted in bias.

Human nature leads you to show favoritism towards those you have psychologically placed in your in-group, often with a blind eye to others with exceptional talent, skills, gifts, and contributions that could improve the team as a whole. Those in your in-group will have more in common with you because they already fit into your systems, which have been established for you and for them.

On the other hand, you might devalue the worth or contributions of the people you psychologically identify as being apart from your social safe space—those in your out-group — keeping them at a distance emotionally, making assumptions about them, or excluding them from interactions with your in-group.

If you, as the leader, rely only on your gut feelings to determine who is or who is not valuable on your team, or who should even be able to join the team—and under what conditions—then you could be missing out on some phenomenal talent. Not liking someone's personal characteristics or even not understanding their culture is one thing. But expecting them to change in order to make you feel comfortable is absolutely unacceptable as an Ally Leader.

Many years ago, I learned of a female executive who received her first big promotion. She was going to be part of the leadership team and, as you can imagine, she was excited. The next day, she received a call from one of the leaders on the team who congratulated her on the promotion and encouraged her to reach out if ever she needed assistance. The caller then proceeded to tell her all of the things she would need to change about herself in order to fit in now that she had accepted the position. They suggested she change her hair color, how she wore her makeup, the type of clothes she wore, how she spoke, and to tone down her overall personality to be less enthusiastic and more reserved and professional. Essentially, this executive was telling her that she needed to change who she was. The newly promoted leader was shocked. After giving it some thought, she called the Congratulator in Chief back.

"I so appreciate you calling to congratulate me, and I especially appreciate you offering your assistance," she said. "Now that we've had the call, I do believe that there is one thing I could use your assistance on."

"Absolutely, lay it on me," the caller said, eager to help, "What do you need?"

"If you wouldn't mind," the new executive replied, "I would like your help drafting a letter to decline the promotion."

"What do you mean? Why would you decline the promotion?" the self-appointed Congratulator in Chief asked, shocked.

"Well," said the newly promoted executive, "if I need to change who I am then I'm no longer interested in the position."

Thankfully, word got back to the head boss, who had promoted her in the first place, and he immediately called her.

"I've just heard what happened and I wanted to personally call to tell you not to listen to those who are telling you that you need to change who you are," he said. "It's because of who you are and the incredible work that you've done that I promoted you in the first place. Your work is exceptional and the way that you view and approach challenges is unique and something I believe we could all learn from. I see your unique perspective as a huge benefit to me and the organization." He ended with, "Don't you dare change a thing."

The bias that women and others face in the workplace seems never ending. Women, in particular, are often expected to change in order to fit into a leadership role that was most likely always held by a man. As such, women are expected to show up, act, and lead like the male leaders who preceded them. That is impossible and an unfair expectation.

The bias that creates an environment that suggests people should change everything about themselves in order to fit in is a hindrance to productivity in the workplace. The burden on women in this instance is so heavy, no wonder this quote from the *Barbie* movie became so famous: "I'm so tired of watching every single woman tie herself into knots so that people will like us."

As an Ally Leader, you are responsible for making the change. It is not the responsibility of other people to change for you.

Understand Your Bias and Rewire Your Brain

As an Ally Leader, you need to rewire your brain by challenging yourself to see beyond what you are familiar with; you do this by asking, listening, and learning about others. It will be easy to pay attention to those who are like you, whereas you will need to do a lot of work to positively notice those in your out-group. Do your part to demonstrate an openness to everyone—especially those coworkers who are not like you. Practicing these ally tactics below will help:

1. Notice those in your out-group. This could be people of a different gender, ethnicity, age group, or physical ability. Just notice them and internally acknowledge that they are different from you; no judgment. Ignoring differences does nothing to enhance your Ally Leadership. Everyone wants to be acknowledged and respected for who they are, so do that.

2. Pay attention to the way people show up in the workplace. This is not merely about their professional attire, although that could be part of it. But notice who comes in early and stays late; how well people engage with others on the team and offer valuable help and support; who takes on additional work; who seeks continuing education; and more. Those go-getters have probably always been there right under your nose, but because some of them are part of your out-group, you might not have noticed their exceptional efforts.

3. Spend time with people in your out-group. This isn't to suggest you spend more time with coworkers who are not like you than you do with those in your in-group. The point here

is to engage authentically and be in the mindset of learning. Don't make this hard. Simply be curious, interested, and open. Ask them questions that you don't already know the answers to, listen, and most importantly learn. Here are a few questions to consider:

- If you could change one thing in the world, what would it be?
- What's one thing you'd like to be remembered for?
- If you were a time traveler would you rather go back to meet your ancestors or forward to meeting your descendants?

As a leader, you must understand and accept that people who are not like you are not looking to be more like you—they're looking for you to accept them as they are. They don't have a desire to look, act, talk, walk, or think like you. They do not want to be you. They want to be themselves. They want you to accept them as they are, not as a future version of you. They want to have the same access to the same opportunities everyone does. However, you might not realize this because people tend to conform to what they believe is the norm, essentially mirroring the opinions and positions of the leader.

The people who have psychologically been placed in your out-group will need to "wear the emperor's clothes" or "go along to get along," trying to mimic what they think you prefer in order to have half a chance to be psychologically liked or even noticed by you. Because they are not like you, they will need to do mental gymnastics, over-perform, or over-work to be afforded the same favoritism you unconsciously provide to your in-group.

As a leader, knowing this is a common practice, you should continuously encourage open communication and free-flowing idea exchange so people do not fall into the trap of doing or saying what they think you want to hear. Ask questions that challenge their thought process to encourage individual thinking.

> **People** who are not like you are not looking to be more like you; they're looking for you to accept them as they are.

A huge hindrance of all leadership is bias, both conscious and unconscious. Everyone has some form of bias and not all of them are bad; however, what *can* be bad is not recognizing your bias, which can cause you to make bad decisions.

Conscious biases are feelings and intents that are clear to you. They are thoughts and beliefs that you have made a conscious, intentional decision to adopt. You might dislike immigrants, religious people, or gay people for your own personal reasons, and those biases often lead to prejudicial actions. If you believe that all gay people are hyper-sexual party animals, then whenever you encounter someone you believe to be gay, you might avoid them or make inappropriate and incorrect comments that reveal your bias.

Unconscious biases are stereotypes that affect your decisions in ways you are unaware of. For example, you might think that all Asian people are good in math, technology, and photography. So, if you're on vacation and need a picture taken, you look for the closest Asian person in the crowd, not even realizing why you are seeking out an Asian person for that specific favor. Unconscious bias is the most dangerous because you are unaware that you're doing it. How that can show up for you as an Ally Leader is you might ask the female in the meeting to take notes, or you might unintentionally make inappropriate comments about someone's hairstyle or attire, or you could assume that an employee who uses a wheelchair is unable to perform certain responsibilities.

Other ways unconscious bias can show up in the workplace is that you might mistake the female employee as having a junior role. You might see a young person as lazy or an older employee as incapable. If you work in a medical environment, you might assume a male nurse is a doctor and a female doctor is a nurse. The list goes on and on.

Here are some questions from Baylor University's Implicit Bias Test by Mecia Lockwood, Assistant Director for Leadership Development. These are designed to reveal unknown biases you might have.

- Who are my closest three friends? What similarities do we share (race, social class, etc.)?
- Who are my neighbors?
- When was the last time I noticed a prejudice in myself (conscious or unconscious)?
- What is an environment I find myself most comfortable in? Who else is there?
- When I picture a pilot in my head, what do they look and sound like (race, gender)?
- When was the last time I educated myself about the culture and experiences of another race, religion, or ethnic group?
- When was the last time I took the lead to welcome a person different from myself into an activity, event, or space?

How did you do with this test? Based on your answers, what can you do now? First, sit with your truth and try to understand the why behind your answers. For example, if all your friends are of the same race, gender, and social class and you feel most comfortable in environments when only those who are like you are there, then decide to mix it up. Don't overthink this. There are ample places for you to visit and experience where not everyone is like you. Get out there; there's a whole world that awaits you.

Connecting With People Who Aren't Like You

When you approach this new aspect of your leadership role from a position of honor (not privilege), willingness (not force), humility (not pride), and joy (not misery), you embrace every aspect of it. You "get to" become an Ally Leader, even as you know you "have to." Ally Leadership is both a requirement of today's leaders as much as it is a source of delight, satisfaction, and triumph. This is not an optional thing you can choose or not. You must adopt and practice Ally Leadership consistently if you are to remain relevant.

As an Ally Leader you must be intentional about connecting with people who are not like you. Do not fool yourself into thinking that because you are a nice person or because it's the right thing to do, you will automatically take these actions. You won't. This cognitive process goes beyond the "right thing to do." Much of the change involves you removing your in-group bias by making the unfamiliar familiar.

As you begin your practice as an Ally Leader, you will consistently **A**sk, **L**isten, and **L**earn so you can become the best **Y**ou to those you lead. Here is how you become a true Ally Leader:

Ask yourself a few questions: Do people who are not like you seem comfortable when interacting with you? What are five things that you have in common with each individual who is not like you? What types of struggles have you both experienced? What do you respect about those not like you? How can you spend more meaningful, one-on-one time with individuals in your out-group?

Listen: Learning how to actively listen is a true art form. Active listening simply means that you do not let your mind wander or become distracted, but instead focus one hundred percent on the person speaking, regardless of how different they are from you or whether you agree with them. You use all of your senses to hear them. You listen with your ears and your heart by putting yourself in their shoes. You watch their body language and facial expressions because some of the most powerful words are unspoken. You repeat or rephrase their questions and comments so that you truly understand the essence of what is being said. You will know when you're in active listening mode because you'll find yourself immersed in their world as they speak to you.

Learn: When you listen intently to someone, you learn how to bring out the best in them. You will learn what they need from you in order for them to be more productive. You'll learn how to attract or retain them as top talent, how to communicate your vision and your company's mission and purpose, and how to communicate cross-culturally, making your personal brand a global asset.

You: All of this positions you to take action on things you deem important. In order to have a team that consistently wins, you must first know what makes them winnable, what makes them tick, what they need from you as their leader so they can be more effective. What's going on in their world that has become a hindrance for them? What are they excited about or interested in? Most importantly, how can you use your power and insight to change the situation and help them win? After all, you are the leader; you make things happen.

Whatever you ask, listen, and learn, you then must act on. That's what it means to be an Ally Leader.

When you ask, listen, and learn, you discover new truths about those who are different from you. Most importantly, you learn more about yourself, what triggers you, and new ways to rise as an Ally Leader. The techniques to do all of this are simple, but at the start can seem complex, even intimidating. A few of the most simple techniques include:

1. Think about what you hope to learn. Don't assume anything because one of the main hindrances to Ally Leadership is assumption. When it comes to people, you must judge everyone based on your interactions with them, not on what you have heard or read about the demographics they belong to. What's important to them? What's unique about them? What excites them most about their work or life? How can you help?

2. Ask open-ended questions and stay away from questions that require a yes or no answer. Asking too many closed questions that require only a yes or no response causes people's defenses to go up. They begin to feel as if you're backing them into a corner. Closed questions tend to start with Do, Did, and Are. As an example: "Did you take time off?" Open-ended questions become extremely useful when trying to understand someone and allowing them to open up. Those questions tend to start with How, What, Why, and If. As an example: "What do you like to do during your time off? What's the funniest thing that's ever happened to you? If you could change one thing about the world, what would it

be? What's the hardest thing you've ever had to overcome?" Expect to hear things that do not align with what you have always believed. When that happens . . .

3. Ask follow-up questions to comments that do not make sense to you. Because you are learning something new about someone you're probably not that familiar with, it's common to have your current belief system challenged. When that happens, dig deeper by asking more questions. Do not let the fear of sounding stupid or feeling uneasy stop you from going deeper. Remember, you are seeking to understand.

4. Say "Thank You." After asking questions and learning something new, thank them for taking the time. A simple thank you makes people feel appreciated and gives them the sense that you found the conversation valuable.

5. Ponder. Spend time reflecting on what you learned. What is one thing you learned about them that you didn't know going into the conversation? What's one thing you discovered about yourself because of the conversation?

To get a list of my favorite open probe questions to ask when getting to know someone, visit www.stephaniechung.com/bonus

As you begin your new Ally Leadership journey, you will have to make some adjustments to your typical leadership style and persona. Do not panic. Remember, you are going into this with honor, humility, willingness, and joy. You won't lose yourself; instead, you will gain the respect of your entire team, particularly those who are not like you. You will become the undisputed hero of your team.

What I Learned From the Damsel in Distress

Early in my role as a VP, I had an employee who stretched my patience on an ongoing basis. We'll call her Melissa. In all honesty, I did not like Melissa. She was a completely different personality from me and drove me bonkers. She often played a damsel in distress who needed to be saved from her own bad decisions. An absolutely beautiful young lady, she struck me as someone who spent way too much time watching reality TV because she seemed to always bring the drama.

She was one of those hires that you almost instantly regret hiring. You know the type. The ones who demonstrate something slightly off during their onboarding and you think to yourself, *Uh-oh, what have I done?* Within seven days of hiring her, I was already thinking of an exit strategy.

On one cool, crisp Thursday morning, I stood in the lobby of my hotel in Monterrey, California, awaiting the transportation vehicles that were assigned to take my team and me to the Concours d'Elegance, one of the world's most prestigious car shows. This show was a massive display of luxury, where some of the world's most impressive—and most expensive—cars were on exhibit. All of the automotive companies were in attendance to show off their latest designs. As a private jet company, it only made sense that we would be there as well, since many private jet flyers are also car enthusiasts. It was 7 a.m. and we needed to be at the venue before 8 a.m. to set up. Between traffic, finding parking, and then walking the half-mile to our booth, leaving at 7 was cutting it close.

As I stood there in my neon green branded shirt and my white capri pants—an outfit dreamed up by our marketing staff—I thought about the day ahead. Today was going to be fun, but long. We would entertain guests at our booth all day, then host a dinner party later that night.

My team began arriving in the lobby to join me, each slightly hung over from the night before. I quickly took a headcount before we all piled into our vehicles to make sure we left no one behind. I counted and recounted the group, growing frustrated with each passing second because one neon green-shirted person was missing. *Who am I missing? Ah, the new girl, Melissa.*

Melissa had joined the team less than a week prior and she was nowhere to be found. As we sat patiently in the minivan waiting for Melissa, I watched the clock hit 7:10. My concern shifted to disappointment, then to anger when I saw her calmly strolling towards us late . . . and out of uniform.

Before she joined the group, I met her halfway.

"Why aren't you in uniform?" I asked.

"Well, last night at dinner we all talked about how much we thought these shirts were hideous, so I decided not to wear it," she cheerfully responded.

Gritting my teeth and reminding myself to breathe, I asked, "So, let me get this straight. You have your shirt, and you've just decided, after working here a week, that you're going to ignore the event team's uniform requirement and instead do things your way? Is that correct?"

Sensing my tension, and now seeing me and all of her peers wearing the same hideous neon green shirts, her face turned bright red, her shoulders dropped, and her voice quivered as she sheepishly apologized.

Pausing for a moment while I counted to ten, I leaned over and whispered to her, "You have three minutes to go upstairs and put that shirt on. If you're not back in three minutes, we're leaving you."

There are times as a leader when you don't actually like a person you are responsible for leading. This is a bit of a taboo subject, but let's have the conversation. Not everyone on your team is someone you want to hang out with, and that can sometimes make Ally Leadership . . . complicated.

My relationship with Melissa was complicated. After the neon green shirt incident and a few others, I thought long and

> **Your job** is not to like everyone. Your job is to respect everyone, to develop and to lead everyone despite how they differ from you.

hard about her, and I even questioned her value and contributions to the team. She was a talented and kind person, but she lacked good judgement. Her professional maturity needed some work, but overall, she had the potential to become an asset to the company.

As the leader and decision-maker, it would have been easy for me to let her go and chalk it up to her not being a good fit. However, I wouldn't have been acting as an effective Ally Leader. My not being emotionally motivated to connect with her was my issue more than it was hers. I was the leader, and as such, the responsibility was on me to try to find a way to make the relationship work and help her improve professionally. I decided to try a different approach.

I often spent one-on-one time with my direct reports. Because our relationship was so strained, I often found excuses to limit how much one-on-one time Melissa and I had together. Without a doubt, I knew I made her nervous and she probably knew that she drove me bonkers. Effectively leading people who are not like you is one thing. Leading people you don't like adds another layer to the already complicated relationship. As an Ally Leader, you must learn to do both.

To help resolve my tension with Melissa, I had my assistant book me a flight to Nashville, where Melissa was located, so she and I could have lunch. When I arrived at the restaurant, I saw Melissa at a table near a window, nervously waving so I could see her. As I headed towards her, I quickly reached out my arms to give her a hug and to attempt to calm her nerves. Even though I had told her that I was flying down to take her to lunch, there was no doubt in my mind that she assumed the worst.

As we chowed down on our sandwiches and engaged in small talk, the conversation soon ventured into our personal lives. She told me that when she was a teenager her mother was killed in a car accident, leaving her to be raised by a domineering dad along with two rambunctious brothers. *Wow! A household of men,* I thought.

After hearing her story, my empathy kicked in and many things now made sense. Because she lacked a female figure in her life during those formative teenage years of transitioning from a girl to a woman, she turned to television. Reality TV raised her, taught her how to dress, how to carry herself, and even how to handle her emotions with drama versus introspection.

Instantly, being an Ally Leader to her became not just doable but imperative. I now saw her as someone who was dealt a tough hand and who was doing her best to survive and thrive. I now had a desire to celebrate her rather than just tolerate her, to show her the unspoken nuances needed to maneuver as a female in a male-dominated industry. That lunch forever changed how I saw my role as an Ally Leader.

It's easy to be an ally when you like someone. As a leader, you won't always like everyone on your team nor will everyone on your team always like you, and that's ok. You might not like their lifestyle, religion, accent, or how they carry themselves, but your job is not to like everyone. Your job is to respect everyone, to develop and to lead everyone despite how they differ from you. Your job is to exemplify excellence at the corporate leadership level, to develop talent, to encourage great ideas and innovative thinking, and to ensure the company's bottom line is supported.

You do all of this because you have the experience, knowledge, and emotional intelligence to do so. And you do it all while supporting those within your in-group and those in your out-group. That is Ally Leadership.

KEY TAKEAWAYS

- ALLY stands for Ask, Listen, Learn, and You take action.
- Realize that your brain automatically places people in your in-group and out-group.
- Understand your bias.
- Increase your in-group by asking, listening, and learning about others.

TAKE ACTION

- Invite someone "who is not like you" out for coffee and practice being an ALLY.

WHAT'S IN IT FOR ME? THE ROI OF EARNING ALLY LEADERSHIP

WHEN I SPEAK TO AUDIENCES about the journey to discover the Ally Leader within, a common and understandable question arises: What's in it for me? It's ok to ask the question. Remember, this is a guilt-free book.

On the surface, it may appear like there's nothing in it for you in doing all this work to be an Ally Leader. It might seem like this is all about other people. They're the ones who benefit from being led by someone like you, who—once you've done the work—understands and supports them in an equitable way, where everyone wins.

But you cannot approach this with a self-righteous attitude that suggests doing this work makes you better than anyone else. It does not. You also cannot enter this work with the thought that you are doing it because it's "the right thing to do." Going through the motions of "doing the right thing," with no emotional connection will not make it stick.

Think about your health. We all know "the right thing to do" but seldom do we do it. When is the last time you drank eight glasses of water, ate five servings of vegetables, worked out, had no sugar, salt, or dairy, took your vitamins, and got eight hours of sleep? Unless you've had a health scare, it's probably been a minute, right?

Ally Leadership is no different. Like your health, you must approach this new level of leadership with the end in mind. As you ask, listen, and learn about people who are not like you, consider how that will change you. How will that change your interaction with your employees/colleagues? Once you begin to expand your understanding of others, how will that change your world?

Ally Leadership is an intentional process to amplify your position as a leader. You deliberately expand your leadership role for the betterment of those you lead and for the company you lead. You consciously demonstrate the courage and willingness to move from "I don't give a damn because this doesn't impact me, so I'll make no changes" to "Hmmm, this isn't right, let me learn more" to "Wait, this does impact me, and I'm going to do my part to change it."

You're in the driver's seat. You're in control. But you have to approach this work from the place of wanting everyone to win, including yourself.

So, what's in it for you?

Being an Ally Leader adds tremendous value to your work and your life, and helps you win. You get to keep winning, as you always have, and you get to develop other winners, other leaders. Essentially, you are multiplying yourself, your skills, your approach, and your impact. The world is rapidly changing, and you are an important part of the change. You bring something unique to the table.

As a leader, your day-to-day responsibilities are focused on putting energy into activities that will yield immediate results, things that benefit you, that support the overall goals and objectives of the company, and that help you advance in your career. Being an Ally Leader does not subtract from any of this; it only multiplies it.

The ROI of being an Ally Leader is that you get to:

- gain a competitive advantage over your counterparts because diverse teams outperform traditional teams
- become a more marketable leader by knowing how to lead all God's children

- increase your income potential because you have created a high-performing team
- move forward and not be left behind as the marketplace continues to shift and expect more from its leaders

Vulnerability: Your Secret ~~Weapon~~ Strength

The key to making Ally Leadership work for you, particularly in the beginning, is understanding that you will have to be vulnerable. As with all things in life, when you learn something new, you will have to be ok with not knowing everything at the onset.

Thirty years ago, when I started out in my career, I had a very brief stint working in the cosmetics industry. A friend of mine who was a behavioral specialist reached out to me regarding one of her patients, who was interested in working in the cosmetics industry and wanted to pick my brain about the pros and cons of it. The patient was transgender. Thirty years ago, I knew nothing about the transgender community; I had never even heard the word.

Once I agreed to the meeting, I asked my friend to give me a quick run-down on what exactly it meant to be transgender. I wanted to have as much knowledge as I could so as not to totally embarrass myself. My friend loaded me up with the science behind the psychology and physiology of being trans; however, nothing could prepare me for the sociological aspects of it all.

We agreed to meet for lunch, and when I arrived at the restaurant, I could tell the place was packed just by the overflow of the parking lot. When I checked in, the warm, energetic hostess walked me to my table in center of the restaurant. I could feel the buzz of the place and the power lunches in full throttle.

As I sat at the table, head down in the menu waiting for my guest, there was a sudden, awkward silence. In an instant, every conversation had stopped, silverware was no longer clinking, and every wait staff stood frozen in their tracks. It was as if someone pressed pause in the restaurant. I looked up to see what was going on. As I glanced around the room, I could see everyone's mouths open and their heads turned towards the door. They were all staring at my guest, Taylor, as she was escorted to my table.

I stood up to greet her and introduce myself. The silence in the restaurant was absolutely deafening. As she sat down, I noticed the stares of the other restaurant patrons. Taylor was still physically going through her transition. She stood about five feet ten inches and was professionally dressed in a black pantsuit. Her hair was in a ponytail and her makeup was flawless. As we sat and chatted during our 90-minute lunch, I couldn't help but notice the happenings around us. I'm sure Taylor noticed as well.

Some of the wait staff were in the back pointing, giggling, and making fun of Taylor, while many of the patrons whispered and continued staring. That epitome of a hostess went from all smiles to blatant eye rolls whenever she passed our table. As a person of color, I am all too familiar with the energy directed towards you when no one else in the place looks like you, but the energy and hostility that was being directed towards Taylor was next-level. It was cruel.

As Taylor and I munched on our salads, the conversation eventually evolved from makeup to life in general. The more I watched, heard, and experienced the snickering behind Taylor's back, the more my heart wept for her. Ignorance typically comes from a lack of understanding and, to be honest, I too lacked understanding in this scenario. This was unknown territory for me. So, I decided to ask Taylor's permission to ask questions, listen, and learn about her and her journey.

My goal was to be thoughtful with my questions versus terrified to ask the wrong questions. It's been my experience when trying to connect with people who are not like me that it's important to be respectful. Most people would prefer a bad question in good faith rather than to not have people talk to them at all. So, the first question I asked was: "What questions are off limits?"

Surprised that I would even care, Taylor told me about her childhood, and she even showed me a picture of Michael, the person she was before she transitioned. Michael was a handsome, blonde-haired, blue-eyed guy who exuded that "boy next door" appearance. Looking at the person in the picture and then the person sitting in front of me was interesting. The piercing blue eyes were the same, yet they seemed to be filled with both hope and hopelessness, exhilaration and exhaustion.

As I looked into Taylor's eyes, I couldn't help but think of God and wonder how he would feel if he were sitting at the table with us. Would he be pleased with me asking questions, listening, and learning? Would he be disappointed with the patrons and wait staff who were judging and casting hate? Would he be pleased with the decisions Taylor had made?

I learned a few things from that experience. One is that everybody has a story. Michael was a good-looking kid who grew up in a loving family and was upper-middle class. By society's standards, Michael had it all, yet was uncomfortable in his own skin. As Michael became Taylor, she went through a number of surgeries and hormone therapy just to try to feel "normal." As Taylor explained to me, it was as if she had the mind and mannerisms of a female but was housed in a male body. It was confusing for her and her family as they tried to figure it all out. Taylor and her family lost friends and loved ones as they were shunned from their inner circle.

That experience taught me that I'm ok having uncomfortable conversations. To this day, that was by far one of the most unique conversations I have ever had. Taylor graciously allowed me to load her up with question after question because she knew that I was coming from a place of genuine curiosity, not judgment. Little did I know that learning how to have uncomfortable conversations would eventually become my professional superpower.

The last thing I learned was how self-righteousness can pop up and take over an environment in an instant. I often wonder how I would have acted had I not been the one meeting with Taylor, but instead was a bystander in the restaurant that day. Would I have been one of those staring, pointing my finger, and laughing out loud, or would I have paid no attention? How would I have engaged in the conversation with others at my table about Taylor's presence? Would I have laughed along with them or remained quiet and not participated in the laughter; or would I have been brave and shut down the negative conversation. How would you have handled it?

Ally Leadership is both a head and a heart issue. Some allyships are easier to unpack than others. Don't let the fear of making a mistake stop you from trying. Approach each situation with a sense of sincere curiosity and authenticity. As you acknowledge your vulnerability, you will begin to show and share your lack of knowledge or insecurities. Do not see this as a weakness. Everyone has insecurities; your employees and coworkers do, your spouse does, and your children do.

As a leader, you might not realize that those who surround you—especially people who are unlike you—know that you have insecurities. Sometimes, they know what those insecurities are before you do. The problem is when you do not acknowledge, show, and share your insecurities, the rest of your team feels like they have to ignore or avoid what they already know about you. This can place them in a position of pretense, as in "The emperor has no clothes," the short story in which everyone knows the emperor is naked but feels like they have to pretend otherwise; in short, the emperor is exposed in front of the whole town but is the last to know. Pretending is no way to win as an Ally Leader.

The feelings of not knowing, being vulnerable, being subjected to scrutiny, and perhaps feeling isolated are all things gay people, women, people with disabilities, and people of color feel on a frequent basis. They maneuver those feelings daily, if not hourly, and you can, too. As you become more efficient at Ally Leadership, you will soon see that vulnerability often makes you more impactful as a leader.

As you prepare for the feelings that will come from being vulnerable, accept and welcome them. Lean in and face those emotions. They might seem unfamiliar and foreign at first, but they are there to help you become a better leader. Don't quit when times get hard. Remember, you want to win. Facing and embracing your vulnerabilities is the way forward.

Another critical part of moving forward is taking action, much like I did in my engagement with Taylor. Take some kind of action to improve your knowledge and practice the Ally Leadership skills of asking, listening, and learning. To do this, you will need to shed some old beliefs and behaviors. You might not think you have mindsets that block your ability to be an effective Ally Leader, but you do; we all do. Moving from where you are to where you need to be as an Ally Leader takes being honest with yourself and understanding that the transformation can be quite liberating.

Becoming an Ally Leader is not an option for leaders who want to remain relevant. And although it is a requirement for leaders of the future, it doesn't have to be hard. Treating people the way you want to be treated is what it's all about. Be brave, be vulnerable, be attentive, and most importantly, be vocal. To begin, begin.

How Do You E.A.R.N. Ally Leadership Status?

Ally Leadership is not a title you can bestow upon yourself; it must be earned. In the same way that you don't get to just decide you're a nice person or that you're someone who is fun to be around, others must decide you're a true Ally Leader. Although your heart might be in the right place, it is the actions you take, the observations and perceptions of others, and the impact you make that lend credence to your title as an Ally Leader.

Leaders need to elevate their skills to effectively lead all people in today's workforce. This requires work, commitment, and courage. Why courage? Because courage demands that you show moral strength in the face of difficulty. Leading people who are not like you can be difficult. You will be flung out of your comfort zone—not placed, eased, or moved out, but flung out. Being flung means you are cast out, headfirst. Being courageous means you're going in heart first.

With the onslaught of demands placed on leaders these days, the thought of learning something new in order to "just do your job" might sound exhausting. The good news is, earning your place as an Ally Leader won't require you to adhere to some type of complex checklist, it will only require you to awaken the gifts you already possess. Thankfully, many of the talents have been instilled in you since birth; they just need to be resurrected. When you approach this journey with an excitement to discover the "unknown" (people not like you), all while rediscovering parts of yourself you've forgotten, it can be enlightening and enjoyable.

Ally Leadership, like any true leadership, is a contact sport. Ally Leaders are in the business of developing humans, growing their gifts and talents, and helping them fulfill why they were placed here on earth. You're at the top of the food chain. You're the decision-maker and the one everyone looks to for answers. A lot is riding on you. But all of your know-how and smarts don't amount to much if you don't have the respect of your team.

Earning their respect feels scary, but it doesn't have to be. Here are four pillars to E.A.R.N the respect of your employees and team members, and keep it:

1. **Establish an Environment** where everyone feels seen, appreciated, and psychologically safe.

2. **Assure Alignment** so everyone understands what the company does and why, and they are aware of how their actions impact the overall outcomes for the business.

3. **Rally the Troops** to a common cause larger than themselves. Because nothing unites people faster than having a common cause.

4. **Navigate the Narrows** by tracking, measuring, and monitoring activities so you stay on track.

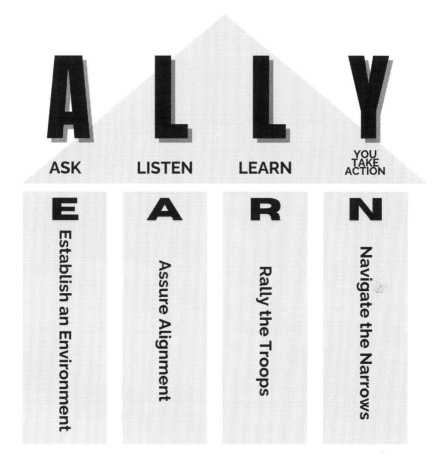

Pillar 1: Establish An Environment Where Everyone Feels Seen, Appreciated, and Psychologically Safe

"Stephanie, I'm scared! I think he wants to die. I can tell that he's tired. Can you come see him?"

Tears rolled down my face as I listened to my employee's wife, Kat, on the phone. Her voice was trembling. She was scared. Who could blame her? Her husband, my employee Paul, was supposed to be in the hospital no more than three weeks following his transplant. We were now coming up on three long months. He was having complications; his body was rejecting the transplant, he was eroding, and his will to live was fading.

"Of course. I'll take the first flight out. I'll be there in the morning." I hung up the phone, emailed my assistant to cancel all of my appointments, and ran to pack.

When we landed, I ran through the airport like Usain Bolt to the Hertz rental car counter. Once I located my rental car, I threw my luggage in the trunk and floored it to Stanford Hospital. As I pulled into the parking lot, I took a deep breath and said a prayer: "Lord God, please give me guidance to say the right things that will bless Paul and Kat. I pray that they be strengthened, his body be healed, and that you provide them and their kids with a peace that surpasses all understanding. Amen."

When I walked into Paul's room, fully clothed in the hazmat-looking suit the doctors had put me in to protect his compromised immune system, I saw Paul muster up enough energy to give me a smile. That smile was the best thing I had seen all month.

I sat there with him until the nursing staff booted me out. During our time together, Paul and I laughed, we talked, and we strategized his return to work. My role that day was to redirect his focus, to give him hope for the future, and to give him something else to think about besides death.

Fortunately, a few weeks later, Paul's body began to accept his new organ and he was released from the hospital just in time for Christmas. I'm sure his presence was the best present his family could ever have hoped for.

I often think about this story and wonder why Paul's wife would call me, his boss, to come visit him during such a monumental and personally trying time. Perhaps it was the fact that I got to know Paul and his family quite well during the time he worked at the company. Maybe it was because I established a friendly relationship with his wife and kids because I knew how important they were to Paul. Perhaps it was that I spent time with Paul, I knew him, his likes, his dislikes, his interest and hobbies. Maybe it was because I cared about him as a person, not just because he was my employee but because he was a person first. Maybe it was because I took an interest in Paul's professional development. I asked him questions about what he wanted out of the job, how it would benefit his life, and I listened. Then, I took action by giving him challenging assignments that would help him achieve his goals. Or maybe it's because I made him feel seen, appreciated, and psychologically safe.

As an Ally Leader, establishing a safe environment is job number one. There are many ways to do it, but for me, I tend to put a lot of effort into getting to know my employees and their families. Getting to know people's families tells you a lot about the person, and it's easier to do than you might think. Here are some actions I have taken in the past:

- Take an employee and their significant other out to dinner a few times a year. This provides a relaxed environment where you can get to know them as people.

- Plan one-on-one time with each employee. When you're overseeing a lot of people, you tend to meet with them as a group. The loudest and most persistent voice in the group typically gets the most attention. Meeting with people on an individual basis allows you to hear from each person without the distractions of the group.

- Set development goals at the beginning of the year and meet to discuss the progress of the goal on a quarterly basis. This allows you to "inspect what you expect" so there are no surprises.

- Understand their personal goals, if appropriate. Because I led sales teams for much of my career, I knew what their commissions goals were. Translating how achieving their commissions goals would allow them to achieve and fund their personal goals was very helpful and shifted the quota conversation. One of my sales directors wanted his bonus to pay for a specific type of Harley Davidson motorcycle. So, I had him go test drive the Harley, take pictures on it, get a hard copy quote, and then come back and tell me all about the experience. Guess what I talked about each month with this sales director? It wasn't his quota. Instead, we chatted about how he was tracking towards the Harley, which was essentially talking about his quota, but in terms that meant more to him. See the difference?

- Create situations where each one can teach one. During team meetings, have the more seasoned team members share best practices with the group. This re-enforces their knowledge while growing the knowledge of others. It also does wonders for creating positive team dynamics.

Pillar 2: Assure Alignment Throughout the Team

Ally Leaders are pragmatic about answering employees' most fundamental questions: What business are we in? How does the company make money? Where is the company going? How does what I do impact what we do as a business? Successfully answering these questions on a consistent basis assures that the team is aligned with the mission of the business.

It was June 1st, another ridiculously hot day in Dallas, and time for our quarterly sales meeting. The team and I had come a long way from the glares and blank stares I'd encountered during our first meeting a few years earlier. We'd fully come to embrace our differences and actually wore our uniqueness like a badge of honor. During our quarterly sales meetings, we'd typically review our numbers, our competition, and our strategy for the remainder of the year. Then we would spend the next day doing sales training and some type of team-building exercise. On this particular day, as the team settled into the meeting room, I asked the sales directors a simple question: "Team, how do we make money as a company?"

In typical "sales team" fashion, they responded, "Steph, the company makes money when we sell something, because as the saying goes, 'Nothing happens until somebody sells something.'" With that, they all laughed and high-fived each other, quite proud of their witty response. I smiled knowing that I had walked into that one. The truth was, their answer was partially right; it also was a sign that we were out of alignment.

"Yes, hitting our quota is one way we make money, but there are other ways as well. Your thoughts on the other ways?" Crickets! I wanted them to think outside the box, to go wide and deep, to consider other ways they could use their skills to impact the company. Finally, I filled in the empty space.

"Ok, we also make money off of fuel, aircraft trade-ins, management fees, maintenance fees, and more," I said. The looks on their faces indicated that they had just learned something new. It was at that moment that I decided I would not have an ignorant sales force.

The truth was, my sales team's response was no different than how most sales teams would have responded. It was important to train them to be business professionals, not just salespeople. The next day, I asked the finance department to join our sales meeting and train the team on the various ways we made money, how we spent money, and how that all impacts cashflow and the P&L.

Having them fully understand what business we were in, how the business made money, and how what they did impacted the business was a game-changer. Not just a game-changer for them, but also for their working relationship with the finance department and the profitability of the company overall. Understanding the complete picture changed how they sold the product, how they negotiated the product, and empowered them to quickly walk away from deals that weren't going to be profitable. Assuring alignment sharpened their sales chops and elevated them from sales directors to savvy business professionals.

As an Ally Leader your job is to help grow your team's talents and knowledge. Here are a few specific steps I took to assure alignment on an ongoing basis:

- Changed what I measured. In the beginning, I primarily measured whether they were on target to hit quota. I later measured the profitability of their deals and changed their commission structure to better reward them for the more profitable deals.

- Created unique opportunities for the departments to interact. Whenever the sales team was in town for our quarterly meeting, I would arrange for other teams to join in on our team-building exercises in an effort to build camaraderie and understanding across different areas of the company.

- Implemented Walk-A-Miles. A walk-a-mile is when employees from one department shadow employees from other departments so they can see and experience what others do and how they do it. This helps employees develop a greater understanding of the business and it helps them understand how what they do (or do not do) impacts their colleagues.

- Overly communicated. I increased my communication with my sales team and with other departments so everyone was in the know. They knew what our goals were, how we were tracking, what departments were crushing it, and which departments needed assistance. I would communicate via videos, conference calls, emails, livestreams, and robocalls. I also expected my direct reports to over communicate the same message during their departmental meetings. I purposely did outreach in various ways, knowing that people digest information differently. The goal was to assure alignment so everyone knew what was going on in the business. Equally as important, I wanted to eliminate ever hearing from an employee: "I don't know what's going on."

In an article titled "Alignment is the Cornerstone of Great Leadership," featured on the website ChiefExecutive.net, writer Jack McGuinness states: "Teams that are not aligned experience chaos and dysfunction. [Consequently], time and resources are wasted on issues that fail to drive performance." As an Ally Leader, assuring alignment is a must.

Pillar 3: Rally the Troops

Ally Leaders know that one of the quickest ways to get a group of people fired up is for them to have a common cause. The cause can be inspirational, motivational, educational, or transformational.

"Ok, everybody, it's coming on in five minutes," our marketing rep yelled out to the various departments as she ran from room to room rounding up folks. "Feel free to grab your snacks and head over to the break room. The reporter said they'll be showing the story after the commercial break."

I joined the rest of my employees in the break room and was a bit nervous to see how the story would appear. A week earlier, a TV reporter had done a story on me being named America's first black person to ever lead a major private aviation company. I wasn't nervous because of the piece; I was nervous because I hadn't seen it in advance of my employees seeing it. We were all about to watch it together. Hopefully, I hadn't done or said anything awkward.

As the commercial break ended and the broadcaster welcomed everyone back, I could feel a stillness overtake the room. I took a deep breath and watched the clip with my team. After it was over, something amazing happened. The team jumped to their feet, high-fived, and hugged each other as if they had just won the Super Bowl. The place exploded with big-boss energy!

Relieved that the piece turned out so well and that the team was excited, I exhaled. Standing in front of my team I said, "Sooo, how'd I do? I hope I made you all proud."

One guy yelled out, "That was awesome!"

"Yea, that was incredible!" someone else shouted.

And then I heard something that literally stopped me in my tracks. One of our junior operations guys rushed to the front of the room, gave me a big hug, turned to the team and shouted: "Guys, we just made history!"

"Yeah, we did!" someone else echoed from the back.

Applauses erupted, smiles emerged, and everyone's attitude was full of joy.

There it was, my "aha moment." I had been so focused on what this historical moment meant for me and others like me, that I didn't recognize the impact it would have on my team (people not like me). This historical moment was a celebration for all of us. This was not just my win, this was a win for my board, our CEO, my team, and everyone else who was involved in the company. This was their moment too. The team was so proud of the fact that we were changing the industry and forcing it to be more inclusive.

That moment was the springboard of many more firsts as the team rallied and the results followed. That year, we were voted one of the fastest-growing companies in Dallas by the *Dallas Business Journal.* We were ranked number one in customer service by *Business Jet Traveler.* And we were the first private jet company ever to earn the Human Rights Campaign's (HRC) Best Places to Work designation.

Rallying the troops to a common cause is fun to do. People like to feel like they're working for something bigger than themselves. It gives them a sense of purpose. As an Ally Leader, I often did the following to help Rally the Troops:

- Think of a cause that aligns with your company's goals. In the case above, one of our company's goals was to have an engaged, inclusive workforce. We communicated, tracked, and measured that consistently. We set aggressive goals, and we were vocal about it as a form of holding ourselves accountable.

- Have fun rallying the troops. One year, I visited my cousin while she was studying at the Army's US Military Academy at West Point. Their football team had an upcoming game against the Naval Academy. Whenever students passed each other or one of their superior officers, they would say, "Beat Navy, sir." It gave the cadets a common cause and lightened up the stoic environment around the entire campus. Similarly, one year we had a goal to dramatically increase our renewal numbers. I created a company-wide initiative called Fuel The Renewal. Finding ways to delight the customer so we could earn their renewal business was everyone's focus for twelve months straight. It wasn't uncommon during that time to hear employees greet each other in the hallways with the phrase, "Fuel The Renewal, sir/ma'am."

- Celebrate often. Think back to when you were in high school. How fun were those pep rallies? They were frequent celebrations that brightened up the day. Why not continue those fun diversions in the workplace? Whenever you rally the troops, be sure to celebrate the wins often. Buy lunch for your team or the entire staff. Splurge for ice cream on a hot summer day. Encourage friendly competition among departments and teams. Stop work early on a Friday and host "movie time," complete with popcorn and candy. Invite employees to bring their spouses, children, or pets to work if appropriate. Opportunities and ways to celebrate are abundant. Be creative.

- Set the team tone at the very beginning. Whenever I take over a team, the very first meeting I have with them I communicate the same exact message: "On this team, you are each other's keeper. We will either all win together or we will lose together; it's our choice." As an Ally Leader, rallying the troops will be part of your repertoire. Learning how to set the team stage at the onset is a must.

Pillar 4: Navigate the Narrows

This is all about measuring things of importance to ensure you stay on course. It's about inspecting what you expect of yourself and others. As you implement change, it is not uncommon to revert to old habits. In order to keep things moving forward, you must track and monitor your progress. This type of tracking is different because it's about doing and tracking those habits that will eventually earn you trust (and Ally Leadership status) from your employees.

Here are a few things that I've done in the past:

- Each week, I would privately write down one to two things I had personally done to show my allyship to my employees. I kept these to myself. It could be something as simple as bragging about them to my CEO so that their name was on his radar. These gestures helped ensure that I was not all talk and no action. Some weeks, I surpassed my goal and some weeks I struggled; and that was ok. What wasn't ok was if three weeks passed and I had done nothing. That was a clear sign that I was falling back into my routine and that my schedule was hijacking my commitment to seek out Ally Leadership opportunities.

- I found ways to make my team the heroes. I would do this by encouraging (and allocating a budget for) them to attend events or trainings that would broaden their understanding of people not like them. It was important that as I was changing and growing in my Ally Leadership, I found ways for my team to change and grow as well. We were all rising together.

If I learned something new, I would share my learnings with others and I would look for them to do the same. For an example, whenever I was sent to media training, I would come back and share with the team what I had learned. Even though they weren't authorized to speak to the media, them having that skillset could help them in other areas. This helped create an environment of curiosity. It also helped amplify awareness of the actions I wanted repeated. Everyone, not just me, was growing in their understanding of others not like them.

- Education and knowledge were essential in my leadership. I created and led a multi-departmental group which focused on ways to educate and expose the organization to important moments or movements. For example, we taught everyone about the history of the Stop The Pay Gap movement. Not only did we share the information, but we also allowed employees to express their thoughts on why they were supportive. They were able to post videos on our internal Slack channel to get the conversation going. The goal was to show people that allyship can be demonstrated in various ways.

- Different people celebrate different holidays. Often, I would send a celebratory message on specific holidays to colleagues who were not like me but for whom I knew that holiday was important. Think Passover, Ramadan, Chinese New Year, Kwanzaa, etc.

- Every month, I would text a person who was not like me and who I no longer worked with to simply check in and say, "Hope you and your family are well. Let me know if there's anything I can do for you. Cheers!" This simple gesture took me thirty seconds to type and often times there wasn't anything that they needed; however, they knew I was there should anything change. Plus, it served as a reminder that being an ally is a lifestyle not a fad.

These were simple things I did to keep myself focused on being a leader to all. Taking these actions helped me be accountable to myself because my goal was, and has always been, to be a leader of impact for both my employees and for the company.

As an aviation professional, navigation is part of my DNA. As an Ally Leader, it needs to be part of yours too. In aviation, there is a concept called "The 1 in 60 Rule." You will learn more about it later in this book, but for now, just know that it is all about making a course correction when you veer off track. And we all veer off track at one point or another along this Ally Leadership journey. The important thing is to identify when and where you have missed the mark, admit the error, learn from it, communicate with those who need to hear your voice, then correct or adjust your navigation pattern as you move on, better for it.

No one expects you to always be perfect at Ally Leadership. But everyone expects you to try, learn, and improve. The world has a leadership shortage. This is your time to fill the gap. You have been called for such a time as this.

KEY TAKEAWAYS

You must EARN the title of Ally Leadership; you cannot bestow it on yourself.

E – Establish An Environment where everyone feels seen
A – Assure Alignment Throughout the Team
R – Rally The Troops behind a common cause
N – Navigate the Narrows

TAKE ACTION

This week, do two things to show your allyship towards someone not like you.

PRIVILEGE ISN'T A DIRTY WORD

THERE IS NO WAY TO be an Ally Leader if we aren't aware of the areas of our lives where we leaders have privilege.

The word "privilege" triggers defensiveness in some people who feel it suggests they have not worked hard for what they have. But that is not what privilege means.

Privilege is an unearned advantage granted to certain people or groups. Almost everyone experiences privilege in some area. It is out of your control and is usually a social construct that results in a benefit to you, and people like you, because you fit into some socially fabricated belief.

White privilege has dominated the public conversation in recent years—and I'll describe it in more detail in a moment—but there are many other types.

Examples of everyday privilege include:

- an able-bodied person going into a building without concern as to whether there's an elevator

- a religious person expecting that their religious holidays align with their work or school holiday schedule

- a man having the ability to walk down the street without being sexually harassed

- a right-handed person being able to comfortably drive a car with a manual transmission because the car was set up for right-handed people.

You are still a hard worker, a nice person, responsible with your resources, and deserving of your accomplishments. No one can take that away from you. Just understand that privilege, or some unearned advantage, also means that your path was not made *more* difficult because of things like your race, your gender, your mobility, your mental acuity, your distance from power, and the like.

> "Seeking to understand your privilege and practicing ways to adjust your opinion of and engagement with others can help you win in your leadership endeavors.

Privilege also shows up when we think about what we consider "normal." Chances are, whatever is common or customary to you and your way of life is what you think of as normal, and anything else is unusual or abnormal. That covers a multitude of things: the food you eat, the way you parent your children, the way you dress, how you worship, keep your house, celebrate, learn, work, and more. This is basic human nature. However, when you believe your norms are "the only" or "the most appropriate" or "the correct" way to be or do something, that attitude reveals your bias and your privilege.

A trademark of an Ally Leader is using your privilege to help others. Effectively leading people who are not like you requires you to pay attention to areas where your privilege can be mobilized to remove barriers for others, using your voice and that same privilege to help level the playing field. This is equity. The goal is not for everyone to win and you now lose. The goal is for everyone to be in position to win, *including* you.

Recognize Your Privilege

Leaders who are blind to their privilege often develop an insensitivity towards others that threatens to interrupt the empathy required to be an effective Ally Leader.

Those privileged leaders struggle to realize and accept that the very experiences they live each day, while normal to them, are not necessarily normal or accessible to others. That lack of accessibility or experience does not make other people less than them in any way—less intelligent, less worthy, less able, less deserving, etc.— nor does it make them and other recipients of these experiences and privileges better than others.

Seeking to understand your privilege and practicing ways to adjust your opinion of and engagement with others can help you win in your leadership endeavors.

Privilege, or unearned advantage, comes in many forms, and most leaders experience at least one aspect of privilege simply by their role as a leader. Because your life is what you would consider normal, you might find it difficult to identify your areas of privilege. So, let's explore some of those areas.

As you read, be open to these examples of privilege and seek to honestly identify areas where certain advantages are a part of your existence. If you experience any emotions in this area, sit with them and more importantly process them, but avoid feeling guilty, ashamed, or angry. The world isn't made better by you feeling guilty about the advantages that have been bestowed upon you. Instead, consider how your privilege can be used to support others who are not like you, or at least be acknowledged to respect others who do not have the same advantages you enjoy. Among those advantages, let's discuss:

- Proximity Advantage
- Male Advantage

- White Advantage
- Class Advantage
- Ability-bodied Advantage

Proximity Advantage

Proximity as a form of privilege means having access to power and resources, as well as social, economic, and cultural capital. You could say that access and proximity are a form of privilege that often puts leaders at the top of the food chain.

As a leader, you are surrounded by others with similar advantages. The advantage of proximity is not a bad thing, and oftentimes it can yield positive results. Much of life is all about who you know and who knows you. As an Ally Leader, it's important to remember not everyone has proximity privilege. This lack of proximity can show up in various ways.

Perhaps an employee of yours who is poised for advancement didn't grow up among the country-club elite that you might be familiar with. They are unaware of behaviors and faux pas on the golf course, in dining situations, or in appropriate attire. This doesn't make them less than; it is simply an opportunity for you to use your advantage to help them by modeling appropriate behavior, communicating certain standards or guidelines, and inviting them to accompany you into spaces they wouldn't normally be invited into.

Early in my career, when I worked as a brand new outside sales rep at an airline, my boss, Pam, who happened to be a female, decided it was time for her and I to hit the road so she could introduce me to my top accounts. Although I had worked for that airline for several years, I had always been either a uniformed Ramp or Customer Service Agent. Now that I was in sales, this was going to be my first time traveling outside the airport facility and into the city to go meet with clients face to face.

I was beyond excited, mostly because this would afford me the opportunity to spend one-on-one time with my new boss. I admired her so much. She was a tall, picturesque, smart woman who I was excited to learn from. She was a legend in our industry. Her family was well-to-do, and it was clear she came from privilege. She grew up attending elite boarding schools and graduated from one of the country's most respected women's colleges, Wellesley.

Eager to make a good impression, I scraped up what little money I had and purchased my very first suit. It was a beautiful pantsuit and I felt awesome in it. That night I could barely sleep due to my excitement.

The next morning, I arrived at the office and immediately went to the break room to say good morning to my boss. She looked me up and down and rudely blurted out, "Is that what you're wearing?"

Surprised by her question, I replied, "Yes."

Without skipping a beat, she yelled out to her assistant, "Jill, cancel all of our appointments. I can't take her to see clients dressed like that." She turned, walked back into her office, and closed the door.

Confused and hurt, I went to Jill's desk to ask what I had done wrong. She could see how hard I was trying not to cry. Jill explained to me that ladies wore dresses or skirts, not pantsuits, to meet with clients. How would I know that? Up until this point, I had only worn uniforms provided to me by the company. This "no pantsuit" nonsense wasn't written anywhere; it was just something that those in the know knew about. Jill wasn't the leader, but she showed Ally Leadership traits that day simply by explaining an unwritten rule with patience and kindness.

As an Ally Leader, it is vital to recognize that not everyone is starting from the same place. That is why asking, listening, and learning about your people is so important. A few simple questions would have provided Pam insight into my upbringing. I grew up a military brat surrounded by soldiers. Seeing ladies in dresses wasn't in my proximity. That didn't make me less than Pam, it made me unaware of the norms.

Later in my career, I was on the opposite side of the equation when I used my proximity advantage to help my family.

"911. What's Your Emergency?" said the calm female voice on the other end.

"My husband's had a stroke. Send an ambulance," I said frantically, trying to hold back the tears.

It was November 2020, and our country was in lockdown due to the COVID-19 pandemic. As I looked at my husband's face, which was drooping on the right side, I leaned in to hear him speak, which was all gibberish at this point. I could tell by his eyes that he was scared. I was scared too.

"Ma'am, the ambulance is on its way."

When I arrived at the hospital and checked in with the receptionist, I tried not to panic as they told me that I was not allowed to see my husband due to the COVID restrictions. This was before the vaccine was created, so the hospital staff didn't know who was and was not contagious. The ambulance had driven my husband to the hospital, but at this point I didn't know whether he had survived the journey or not. If he had survived, who was back there fighting for his care or speaking on his behalf?

As I sat on the cold concrete bench outside the hospital, I thought about what life would be like without my husband of thirty-five years. Sam was the one person who knew me best. The person who I laughed with during the good times and cried with during the hard times. The person I vowed to have and to hold during sickness and health. What I wouldn't have given in that moment to hold his hand, look into his eyes, and whisper in his ear, "You're going to be ok."

After three long, excruciating days, I was finally allowed in the hospital to see my Sam. When I entered the room, his eyes lit up. He smiled from ear to ear and reached for my hand. I hugged him tight, squeezed his hand, and whispered in his ear, "You're going to be ok."

Sam couldn't walk, write, or speak; it was difficult for us both, but we had been through hard times before. He remained in the hospital as doctors tried to stabilize his vitals. When they did begin to improve, doctors said they needed to transport Sam to a rehabilitation facility so he could begin the process of relearning how to function and care for himself. They said that time was of the essence and that he'd need to fire up his brain again to reignite those circuits that controlled language, muscle coordination, and memory. Moving Sam to a full-service rehab center became my new mission in life.

At 8 a.m. the day before Thanksgiving, I stood in my pajamas with a coffee in one hand and the phone in the other.

"What do you mean my insurance company is denying our claim and won't give the approval to move Sam to a rehabilitation center?"

If we didn't get him moved that day, we would have to wait until after the long weekend. We'd lose those valuable days. Knowing the impact it might have on his cognitive functions was unconscionable to me.

"Stephanie, I wish there was something else we could do," the doctor said. "We're just as frustrated as you are. The insurance person said that they'll approve for Sam to receive in-home rehab, but they won't pay for him to go to a full-time care center."

Sam's physician had shared with the insurance company his professional opinion that Sam needed full-time care in a facility, but the insurance company had insisted on the in-home option. I could tell by the doctor's demeanor that he was as frustrated as I was, perhaps even more so because his medical credibility was being questioned by an insurance staffer with no medical background, who only cared about saving his company money.

As a person who has reached the highest levels within the private jet industry, I have proximity privilege. People who buy private jets are wealthy. They have connections and they are the movers and shakers of the world's economy. They are society's power players, they run companies both big and small, and it doesn't matter what country they're from,

> **Some** people have to work harder to get what you have been awarded. Don't lose sight of that as you grow as an Ally Leader and engage authentically with those who are not like you.

they're all millionaires and billionaires. In the twenty-plus years that I've been in the private jet industry I have never used my proximity privilege. But in this instance, desperate times called for desperate measures.

I sent out a text to my network, explained the situation, and asked who could help. Within an hour I received a text from an unknown number that simply read, "What hospital and room is your husband in?" I didn't know who the text was from and at that point, I didn't care. I replied to the unknown sender, and within thirty minutes, one of Sam's doctors called me.

"We're not sure what you did, but your insurance company just gave the go-ahead. Sam is being moved to the rehab facility today. Pack him some clothes and meet him there."

The privilege I enjoyed by being in proximity to wealthy people with connections, who could make things happen in a matter of minutes, was a godsend. Yet, even as relieved as I was with the result, I realized that not everyone has that kind of network or influence. How many people face a health emergency and fight with their insurance company to no avail? How many people die, not because they deserve to or because they didn't plan for emergencies or didn't make smart choices or any number of assumptions society makes about them, but because they do not have the privilege of proximity to those who can work around the rules of the system?

The privilege of proximity isn't something to be ashamed of, nor is it something to tout as a badge of honor. However, it is a reality that you, as an Ally Leader, must acknowledge having in order to be real with yourself about the advantages you have that others do not. Admitting your access to other influential people and resources, and facing the truth that not everyone has that same advantage, should sensitize you to the struggles that others face on their journey to success. Some people have to work harder to get what you have been awarded. Don't lose sight of that as you grow as an Ally Leader and engage authentically with those who are not like you.

Thankfully, after five weeks in full-time, intense rehabilitation, Sam was able to come home and was able to walk, talk, write, and care for himself. I often wonder what might have happened to Sam and our family if I hadn't had the network and proximity to privilege I have.

Male Advantage

Male privilege is a set of advantages in society given to individuals based on their gender as male. Subsequently, disadvantages are heaped upon people whose gender is female. Like not being able to take off your blazer in 120-degree heat in the Middle East because, as a woman, you're not allowed to show your skin, which happened to me on a business trip. Or maybe it's the absence of enough ladies restrooms in large facilities like airports and stadiums, therefore creating a line out the door. Or perhaps it's providing a diaper-changing table only in the ladies room and not in the men's room, as if women are the only parents who can or should change a baby's diaper.

Men currently hold an overwhelming amount of power in corporate America. A June 2024 *Fortune* article titled, "The share of Fortune 500 businesses run by women can't seem to budge beyond

10%" states that 90% of the chief executive officer roles at Fortune 500 companies are held by men. In the S&P 100, 92% of the CEO roles are held by men. There is a saying regarding male privilege: "Men have the privilege of being unaware of their privilege." Nothing exemplifies that statement better than a room full of men reacting to an issue focused on women's reproductive rights.

When I exited the plane after a two-hour flight from Los Angeles to Dallas with no wifi, a slew of text messages buzzed in from my phone. One of them was about an emergency meeting being called that night for the executive team. As an executive in the aviation industry, emergency meetings on a Sunday night can mean catastrophic news. Because I had been out of pocket for hours, my mind automatically assumed the worst—that one of our planes had been involved in an accident. Panicked, I hopped into an Uber to head home and dialed into the Zoom meeting.

The team instantly dove into the purpose of the call, which thankfully had nothing to do with any flight stressors. Instead, the call focused on the US Supreme Court's ruling to overturn Roe vs. Wade. When the decision was announced, some of our female employees sought clarity on the company's position on the issue. Because the ruling had come down less than forty-eight hours prior, executive teams like ours at companies across the country were scrambling to make sense of what was happening. There were a lot of decisions to be made. We needed to dissect our insurance plans, connect with our benefits providers to see what adjustments they were making, and figure out our next steps. To say that our positioning was unclear was an understatement.

In their haste to respond to the incoming inquires, my male colleagues had drafted a letter to our employees, paying special attention to our female staff. The letter that this all-male team constructed not only lacked substance, it also lacked insight and understanding of the issues. It was absent of the nuance that only a female perspective would have captured. On what planet did it make sense for a group of men to feel so inclined to draft a letter about women's reproductive rights, with no input from women?

The lack of privilege awareness was deafening and insulting. Rather than ask the female executives to co-create the letter, the men on the executive team instead wrote it themselves and then shared it with the entire leadership team for feedback. Had there been an informed and aware Ally Leader on the team, they would have insisted on getting input during the drafting of the letter rather than feedback after the draft was complete. Sadly, there were none. Their outreach to get feedback was merely an example of performative inclusion, rather than authentic inclusion. Asking for feedback after the draft was already written simply gave those men permission to "check the box" to say that yes, a woman had reviewed their letter.

A better approach for the executive team in this situation would have been to suggest a small group of executives, made up of males and females, collaborate to draft a letter addressing key points of concern for all employees and critical considerations for the company. Because, after all, women's reproductive rights impact both males and females. Once reviewed by the entire team and adjusted based on open feedback by all, the letter could then be shared throughout the company. Instead, the entire letter had to be squashed and rewritten, costing us valuable time in communicating with employees.

A similar scene that illustrates male advantage is played out day in and day out in many corporate settings when a woman or other marginalized person in the meeting wants to speak up and share their insight. Most often, a male who holds a leadership position disregards the input of those on the team who don't look like them.

In these instances, a few things happen: 1) the team member feels marginalized and may be discouraged from participating in the future; 2) the rest of the team assumes the same will happen to them if they speak up, so they don't give their best to the effort; 3) the entire project or company suffers and loses valuable growth potential. In other instances, the one in the leadership position loves the ideas that have been shared and decides to take the ideas and pass them off as his own. This behavior is both ineffective and unfair. It illustrates male privilege because it perpetuates the false narrative that a man's ideas and inputs are superior to everyone else's.

Men are generally less likely to notice unfair treatment towards women because this unfairness does not directly affect them. This could show up when a woman is constantly interrupted by men in a meeting, or when a female colleague's ideas are challenged by men for their worthiness, or when men assume that the women in the meeting will be assigned to take the meeting notes. In these instances and others, there is ample opportunity for men to exercise their Ally Leadership skills. Male Ally Leadership includes addressing inequities, advocating for women, and acknowledging women's achievements both privately and publicly. Seeing your own privilege is usually difficult, but with awareness, intention, and practice, you will begin to notice inequities and opportunities to make change.

Examples of male advantage:
The following statements are excerpts of The Male Privilege Checklist from Peggy McIntosh's article, "Unpacking The Invisible Knapsack," which first appeared in *Peace and Freedom Magazine's* July/August 1989 issue:

- I'm not interrupted by women as often as women are interrupted by men.
- In general, I'm under less pressure than my female counterparts to be thin.

- If I have children, I can expect my wife to do most of the basic childcare (i.e. diapers, feed).

- Decisions to hire me won't be based on assumptions of whether or not I might choose to have a family sometime soon.

- If I'm not conventionally attractive, the disadvantages are small and easy to ignore.

- I don't have to worry about the message my wardrobe sends about my sexual availability.

- My ability to make important decisions, and my capabilities in general, will never be questioned depending on what time of the month it is.

- I can be aggressive with no fear of being called a bitch.

- I have the privilege of being unaware of my privilege.

White Advantage

As researcher Elizabeth Minnich points out in Peggy Mcintosh's study, white people are taught to think of their lives as morally neutral, normative, average, and ideal. Because of this, when they work to benefit others, they see it as work which will allow "them to be more like us," or what many refer to as "normal."

Peggy McIntosh so wonderfully pointed out in her essay that the two words *white privilege* pack a double whammy because the word "white" creates a discomfort among those who are not used to being defined or described by their race, and the word *privilege* gives the impression that they've never struggled. The defensiveness that can accompany these two words can often derail a conversation. Per McIntosh, white privilege does not mean that a white person's accomplishments are unearned. Most white people have worked hard for their success; therefore, white privilege should be viewed as a built-in advantage, separate from one's income or effort.

Many people around the globe have bought into the false belief that white people are the norm and everyone else is unusual. This simply is not true. White people are not the standard for human beings, Americans, smart people, law-abiding citizens, kind people, hard workers, or leaders. Everyone is different from others who are not like them. Moreover, as the world changes and people of different cultures and ethnicities cohabitate, the world is becoming less white and more brown, so to speak, with different cultures merging to create a spectrum of people with blended and varied backgrounds.

Since the 1950s, the population of people who identify as white in the US has been decreasing and will continue to do so, while those who identify with specific ethnic groups have been increasing. According to the US Census Bureau, the population in the United States will be majority-minority sometime between 2040 and 2050. This means that the majority of the population will represent citizens from a variety of ethnicities and cultures that are viewed as minorities when taken individually. Together, however, they will make up the majority.

As cited in the 2018 article titled "What is white privilege, really?" in *Learning For Justice Magazine*, white people often ignore or marginalize mistreatment and discrimination of individuals from different racial, ethnic, or cultural backgrounds. For an example:

- White people are less likely to be followed, interrogated, or searched by police officers because they "look suspicious."

- White people's skin tone will not be a reason people hesitate to trust their credit or financial responsibilities.

- White people are never asked to speak for *all* people of their racial group.

- White people can do well in a challenging situation without being called a credit to their race.

This doesn't make you, as a white person, a bad person; it's human nature to pay less attention to things that don't impact you. However, as an Ally Leader, you are charged with the responsibility of paying attention to inequities within your company, and taking action to create an equitable, fair, and transparent workplace for all.

Following the murder of George Floyd, workplaces across the nation were on alert. Some were concerned that an uprising of angry employees would disrupt the workday. Others went into high gear instituting and expanding their DEI departments and policies. Leaders who were on the outskirts, lacking understanding of the gravity of the social climate, were stunned to learn how that one event impacted their coworkers. Ally Leaders, on the other hand, grappled to connect with their teams and allow them to express their feelings. Many authentic Ally Leaders, however, felt even that wasn't enough.

"Hey Steph, you got a minute?" I could hear my friend Ted on the other line. He didn't sound like his usual self. He sounded distraught.

"Of course," I said. "Are you ok? What's going on?"

After a long pause, Ted, who happens to be white, proceeded to tell me how disappointed he was in himself. He was disappointed in how he had just handled a situation at work which involved his global team.

As part of their company's corporate culture initiatives, all leaders were encouraged to have monthly calls with their teams to check in and see how everyone was doing. With the pandemic and the social unrest that was breaking out around the world, these calls had become more and more important. On his team call, which took place a few days after the murder of George Floyd, Ted shared with his team that he was shaken by everything that was happening in the world. He spent a majority of the call talking about how devastated he was, how upset he was, and how he was losing sleep over it all. Essentially the entire call became about Ted and his feelings.

A call that was supposed to be about how the global team, made up primarily of black and brown people, was doing, turned into an hour-long therapy session on how the white guy was feeling due to all the social injustice he was watching play out on TV. Whereas many of his global team members weren't just watching injustice, but had experienced it their entire lives.

Bottom line, Ted lacked awareness of the privilege he had been given because of the social group he belonged to—white and male. The privilege he exhibited was twofold: 1) The freedom from ever having personally experienced—or even knowing anyone else who had experienced—a similar injustice as that of George Floyd and others reported in the news; and 2) being in position to take control of the entire conversation and making it about his feelings.

For Ted, the sheer thought that a police officer, who is paid to serve and protect, would mistreat another human being was shocking. The thought that this police officer was emboldened enough to kill a man in plain daylight with cameras rolling, was shocking to Ted. For him to have watched 25-year-old Ahmad Aubrey be gunned down like a wild animal a few months earlier by men who weren't even cops was shocking to him as well. For Ted, all of this was unbearable.

What Ted failed to realize was that those things were unbearable for his employees too, but not for the same reasons they were for him. For his black and brown employees, they were unbearable because these incidents happened way too often to them and people they knew. For them, years of mistreatment and the toll it was taking simply because of the color of their skin was intolerable. For them, the fact that it took this long for these types of abuses to finally be caught on camera was shocking. For them, having to live each day just trying to survive being born black or brown was a heavy reality. For them, having to have "the talk" with their kids about how to behave around police because the police weren't always there to serve and protect them was insufferable. For them, having to shrink themselves so that their mere presence didn't intimidate others or provide them with an excuse to beat or shoot them was a heavy burden. That's why they found the latest happenings unbearable.

Ted would have understood all of this had he simply asked, listened, and learned. Instead, he did what many people with privilege do; he made it about himself. Luckily for him, no one embarrassed him on the call. However, a few of his direct reports cared enough to call him separately and provide him with some much-needed feedback.

Lacking privilege awareness and making a mistake doesn't make Ted a bad guy; it makes him human. Same for you and any other Ally Leader. This is not about feeling guilty because you are unable to relate to other people's traumas or experiences. This isn't about trying to make things better by simply saying how badly you feel about a terrible situation. What this is about is minimizing self-centeredness. The world has changed, and it requires that all of us view things from others people's viewpoints. It is no longer acceptable to only view things from your lived experience and then hog up the conversation telling people about how you see things. Your experience is only one viewpoint, not the one and only viewpoint.

A more appropriate approach Ted could have taken in this situation would have been to stick to the script. Meaning the company's objective for the frequent check-ins was to see how everyone else was doing during this time of social and civil unrest. The only way that you'll ever know how people are doing is to ask, listen, and learn, and then you act to change those things that you can. I cannot stress this enough: If you are going to be an Ally Leader, you must shift the attention from you to the people you lead—their needs, their concerns, and their life, not yours.

In the absence of acting appropriately, the best course of action for Ted was to learn and improve. Learn from the mistake, apologize for the error, and then move on. You will find that most people will give you grace, especially if they see that you're trying to understand your privilege and use it for the betterment of all. Where they will not give you grace is if you say that your privilege doesn't exist and you just tout yourself as being better than everyone else. Ted learned a valuable lesson that day and by doing so became a better leader, an Ally Leader, for his team.

Consider these examples of white advantage that suggest whiteness as the "norm":[1]

- White people can criticize the government without being seen as a cultural outsider or a threat.
- White people can see the police as a source of safety not danger.
- White children will be given books in school that testify to the existence of their race.
- Being able to accept a job without worrying whether or not there will be people of your own race there.
- The ability to go shopping without being followed around by suspicious employees or security guards.
- You're never told you're "surprisingly" pretty, smart, or well-spoken for a white person
- You have the privilege of learning about racism instead of having to experience it.

---

[1] Niloufar Haidari, "50 Examples of White Privilege to show family members who still don't get it," Vice.com, June 9, 2020. https://www.vice.com/en/article/4ayw8j/white-privilege-examples

Class Advantage

All I could think was: *I've never been this hot in my entire life. Good grief, I feel like my face is melting off.* It was August 2019 and my colleagues and I had just landed in Qatar. I was excited to be traveling to this part of the world as I had heard that the country was magnificent.

My colleagues and I met in the hotel lobby, where I gave everyone a pep talk about how monumental this trip was and how we were going to crush it this week. As we all chatted about the best way to get to our appointment, we realized that our meeting was only one block away and agreed that walking the block would be much faster than trying to figure out how to arrange for transportation. Besides, it was only one block.

As we exited the hotel, I felt the heat immediately slap me in the face. *This is going to be the longest one-block walk of my life.* Every ten steps or so, one of my male colleagues removed his suit jacket, which revealed sweat stains already soaking through their dress shirts. *How nice for them,* I thought. *I can't even remove my jacket because the culture here doesn't allow women to show their skin.* By the halfway point, everyone stopped talking and all I could hear was heavy breathing. The stifling heat was literally sucking out our energy, and I was beginning to feel woozy.

Finally, we arrived at our destination. The walk was less than five minutes, but we looked like we had all just finished a triathlon. We were hot, sweaty, and out of breath. Before heading to our meeting room, we all stopped at the restrooms to freshen up as best we could.

Once in the meeting room, we were greeted by a gentleman who offered us coffee and tea. The thought of consuming anything hot was an unbearable one. Containing our urge to laugh in this guy's face, we kindly declined the hot beverage and asked for cold water. He obliged. As we sat waiting for the other attendees to arrive, I struck up a conversation with the gentleman who was kind enough to keep loading us up with water. I learned that he was from India, that he had a wife and child back home, and that he had been living in Qatar for a few years. He was kind, soft spoken, and extremely attentive to our needs. I enjoyed learning about him.

Eventually, our host arrived. Following handshakes and introductions, everyone sat down to begin the meeting. Just then, our host noticed that none of us had coffee cups in our hands.

Frustrated, he shouted, "Sanjay, did you offer them coffee?

Sheepishly, Sanjay whispered, "Yes, Sir, I did."

"Why don't they have coffee?" he asked, standing up and exerting a much more aggressive tone.

Surprised by the sudden turn of events, and a bit shocked by the hostility towards Sanjay, we all stepped in to assure our host that Sanyjay had offered us coffee, but that we had chosen water instead. Undeterred by our response, our host, now in Sanjay's face, again asked, "Why don't they have coffee?"

"Would you like coffee?" Sanjay whispered, looking scared for his life.

Confused and extremely uncomfortable with this entire exchange, we all said, "Yes, yes, we'll have coffee, thank you." With that, Sanjay left to fetch us some hot coffee. None of us wanted the coffee but we did want to give Sanjay a reason to leave the room as we didn't know what the next round of questioning would bring him.

I wish I could say that was the only time I had such an awkward encounter while interacting with the servants in Qatar, but the very next day I experienced an almost identical experience while attending another meeting. This time it wasn't a Sanjay, it was a Naomi. A beautiful young woman from Africa.

The next day, when I entered the meeting room and met with my meeting host, before she could even begin to lay into Naomi as to whether she had offered me a hot beverage, I beat her to the punch.

"The hospitality this morning has been impressive," I said. "As soon as I walked in, Naomi was kind enough to offer me hot tea. It was literally the best tea I've ever had. Thank you so much Naomi for your kindness. I look forward to seeing you again before I leave."

And with that, I gave her a big smile and made a small gesture indicating she was free to leave the room. There was no way I was going to let Naomi get screamed at in my presence.

Privilege can come in many forms. In the United States we tend to think of privilege in terms of race, gender, or socioeconomics. In other countries, privilege may be the same or different. Regardless of where you reside, Ally Leadership is about understanding that those not like you have different lived experiences. Some of the experiences are easy to comprehend, others not so much. My experience in Qatar showed me 21st century servitude. It made me uncomfortable.

Ally Leadership—in any country—requires action. Although I cannot change how Qatar operates, I can change how I operate while there. After the unexpected Sanjay experience, I was more prepared for the Naomi situation, and I brought my Ally Leadership front and center at the start of that meeting.

As an Ally Leader, sometimes you taking action won't involve a colleague, family member, or friend; sometimes it will be for a stranger, a fellow human being. Regardless of who it's for, taking action is what Ally Leaders do.

Ability-bodied Advantage

Diversifying a company is easy; making a company inclusive is hard. Most companies review their talent pipeline and then put measures in place to increase diverse talent. That's not complicated. What's complicated is revising your internal processes which inherently have bias woven within. Making systemic adjustments is not for the faint of heart.

When I received a call asking if I could assist in finding transportation for a traveler who was wheelchair bound, I welcomed the request. The company, whose high-level executive needed this essential service, was having difficulty chartering a jet because none of the jet companies were equipped to accommodate the needs of a traveler in a wheelchair. Thankfully, I was able to find a company that had experience in this area. Instead of deciding to refuse the request and "jump ship" because this was going to be hard, this company instead leaned in.

We first had to find a jet that had a large enough baggage compartment to store the wheelchair. We then needed to secure a medical service provider that had the equipment and capabilities to lift the traveler onto the aircraft, at both her departure and arrival cities. We then had to confirm that her husband could and would dismantle the wheelchair and remove the battery so it could go in the back of the aircraft with the luggage. The traveler, who is a world-renowned speaker and advocate for people with different abilities, rarely travels. She tends to do her speeches virtually, and I completely understand why.

The bias that was directed towards us for trying to make this trip happen was unbelievable. I can only imagine the feelings she had encountered in the past for being perceived as an "inconvenience." To make this trip happen, we had to deconstruct and then reconstruct a new system.

Imagine reviewing all of your internal policies from a black or brown person's perspective; from an LGBTQ+ person's perspective; from a female perspective; from a religious person's perspective; and yes, from the perspective of a person with different abilities. Doing so takes less time and effort than you might imagine, and the positive benefits can be exponential.

Instead, companies expect diverse employees to acquiesce to a system, process, and culture that is not set up with them in mind. After the sheer exhaustion of trying to function within a system that wasn't designed for everyone—and is unwilling to do the work to adjust—all parties then give up. The diverse employees quit and the leadership is left scratching their heads and asking themselves, "What the heck happened? We hired diverse talent. We welcomed them with open arms. We showed them how we do things around here. We thought we did everything right. We're not sure what else we could have done." And with that, everyone moves on and things return to the status quo.

Systemic adjustments are not easy. Making people feel included, or like they belong, isn't easy. You know what's easy: saying you're a company that embraces diversity, equity, inclusion, and belonging (DEIB) and then not addressing your internal systems to back up your statements. And although this performative inclusion behavior might seem easy, it actually results in tarnished corporate goodwill, unsatisfactory customer experiences, low employee morale, and lost revenue.

Here is a different approach to consider. The above strategy relies on the one-way "I" approach: I hired them, I showed them how things are done around here, etc. Instead, do the "We" approach. Create employee resource groups (ERGs) for your company. These groups can include your female, religious, people of color, disabled, and LGBTQ+ employees. Assign an executive to each group, or volunteer to be the executive sponsor for one of the groups. ERGs can help establish a sense of belonging among your diverse colleagues, while informing other employees of the concerns, interests, and knowledge of those diverse groups. They are also beneficial to help review the current policies in place and provide a different perspective on the pros and cons of the policies.

You can also bring in monthly speakers to address all employees to help educate and bridge the knowledge gap when it comes to cultural differences. Try creating an uncomfortable conversation series that allows all employees an opportunity to express their thoughts and share insights with each other. Consider establishing a Diversity Council to serve as your internal brand ambassadors who partner with the different business functions to educate them and celebrate cultural holidays. The goal is to transition from an "I" approach to a "We" approach. The "We" approach allows everyone to participate in a system that is designed by and for everyone.

Solidarity and Social Capital

The unspoken code of solidarity among people with privilege can often feel like a blanket of protection. In reality, it serves as a shroud of ignorance allowing complicit thoughts and behaviors rather than encouragement to stand bold and strong as an Ally Leader.

Being in solidarity with those in your in-group—those in the same gender, economic class, sexual orientation, or cultural or religious background as you—basically means that you would never embarrass each other by creating discomfort for them by pointing out an act of prejudice, racism, sexism, bias, or bigotry. Instead, you would keep quiet to remain in solidarity with each other, which protects your advantage and privilege.

Social capital is the intangible reward you get by staying quiet in the midst of the injustice against people who are not like you, particularly when your in-group witnesses your silence. Demonstrating your solidarity to your in-group in this way feels safe because you are included, you're an insider, a team player. This social capital also earns you opportunities within a corporate setting.

Depending on your social or economic standing, you might actually enter the corporate setting with a pocket full of social capital you didn't even earn, an accrual of sorts that you have collected over time; it just came with the territory you were born into. Yes, there's that privilege again. By refusing to speak up or take action against an injustice, while those in your in-group also remain complicit, you silently communicate an agreement with the injustice. As leadership coach Paul Scanlon says: "Silence is not benign, it's malignant because you become complicit."

Social capital and solidarity are gained in situations where you, the white male for example, sit in the midst of the other fellas when one guy tells the sexist or racist joke. It's a private setting, so what's the harm, right? The guy who tells the joke is usually the same guy who doesn't think twice about talking bad about people behind their back, thrives on humiliating people in public, asserts his power by belittling others, or has an overall belief that he's better, smarter, and more entitled than everyone else. You know that guy. We all do.

The problem is that this guy doesn't tell those jokes to everyone; he only tells those jokes or makes those comments to people in his in-group because he believes they understand and feel the same way. But you don't feel the same way. You're not "that guy," and every time you hear one of those jokes you feel uncomfortable, but you don't say anything. Instead, you walk away, hoping to distance yourself from him, and convince yourself that you're better than "that guy" because you choose not to participate.

This isn't just a white guy thing; what about the person of color who tells a mean-spirited racist joke about a non-ethnic person? Or the person who mocks another person's accent or culture? Or, that social capital might show up when you, as a straight person, are confronted with someone whose sexual orientation is different than yours, like the people in the restaurant who stared and whispered to their peers as my lunch guest, Taylor, walked in. Rather than insist that their cohort mind their own business and remain focused on the purpose of their gathering, they all engaged in the rudeness.

Solidarity among those in your preferred political party or other in-group rears its ugly head when one person openly disagrees or behaves differently, and the rest of the in-group rallies to make that person feel as if they have done something wrong. You watch silently as the group berates or belittles the other person, but you remain distant and allow the negative discourse to continue.

Here's the thing: silence is acceptance. By not saying anything, you are basically saying that you're down with sexism, racism, and every other ism, and you're signaling to "that guy" or to the group that you're "that guy" too. But you're not that guy and no one, and I do mean no one, is going to give you any credit for walking away. You only get credit for doing something about it. That's what Ally Leadership is; it requires action. Author Brian Tracy says: "It is not what you say or hope, or wish, or intend, but only what you do that counts. Your choices tell you unerringly who you really are." The same is true for Ally Leadership.

KEY TAKEAWAYS

- Everyone has privilege, acknowledge yours.
- Think about an uncomfortable scenario when you said nothing but wished you had.
  - What was the situation?
  - How did it make you feel?
  - If you had to do it over again, what would you have said?

TAKE ACTION

Today, choose one simple way to use your privilege for someone else's benefit.

ALLY LEADERSHIP:
THE NEW FRONTIER

BEING AN ALLY LEADER IS all about showing versus telling. You might tell yourself that you're an ally, but being an Ally Leader requires action. Truth be told, if you *show* your Ally Leadership then you will never have to *tell* anyone about it because they will be able to see it for themselves. As the saying goes: "Actions speak louder than words."

Forging true Ally Leadership can be likened to building muscle. When you decide to get healthy you don't have to go looking for muscle; you already have it within you. However, you may not know how to build it, strengthen it, tone it, or create muscle memory. That's why you need the guidance of a fitness coach or personal trainer.

Most human beings have Ally Leadership built in. We were born for human connection. We instinctively know the difference between right and wrong. We know that kindness is better than meanness, being gracious is better than being cruel, sharing is better than being stingy, and openness is better than being shut off or shutting others out. Given your innate characteristics, becoming an effective Ally Leader doesn't require nearly as much work or adjustment as you might think. There is no twenty-step process or some checklist you have to review each day to stay on task. But you might need a bit of guidance to navigate certain situations.

"Steph, Keith wants you to join a call with him today at 1 p.m."

The email was from my CEO's executive assistant.

"Ok, do I need to prepare for the call? What's the call about?" I replied.

"No need to prepare. There will be other people on as well. The call will center around fundraising."

Fundraising? That's not my specialty, I thought.

A few minutes before the call, I logged into Zoom only to see some of the who's-who of white male millionaires. My CEO quickly welcomed everyone, introduced me, provided some background as to the purpose of the call, and then welcomed the guest of honor, Professor Johnson. Professor Johnson was a distinguished-looking black man who taught at one of the most recognized and renowned learning institutions in the country. Immediately, I understood why I was on the call. I was there as a friendly face, moral support, an ally if you will, for Professor Johnson.

I could tell that Professor Johnson was not only good at what he did but he also wanted the best for his students. Professor Johnson shared why he thought his students and the university as a whole were at a competitive disadvantage due to their lack of diversity. He shared research highlighting disadvantages that students experience when their world is surrounded by social sameness. He also talked about the negative impact the handful of minority students faced due to the lack of diversity on campus.

Professor Johnson's presentation was impressive. On board with what the professor had said, one of the attendees asked if Professor Johnson could share his wish list of what he would like to see happen and what he needed in terms of funding to make the changes happen. I think the professor was pleasantly surprised by how quickly the attendees offered their support. He laid out his vision and his very well-thought-out execution strategy. With that, the millionaires all nodded in agreement and gave their verbal support to fund the project. Millions of dollars were raised during that twenty-minute call. Turns out the millionaires all had kids who went to that university, and they didn't want their kids unprepared for the real world.

These men all wanted everyone to win, especially their own kids. They sent their kids to that university because of its academic programs. It's a safe bet that they didn't think about its diversity stats because they didn't have to. Having diverse students on (or not on) campus didn't impact them, or so they thought.

Education isn't found only in books. The best education we all have tends to come from the school of life. Hearing the professor lay out the educational disadvantages their kids might encounter due to their sea of sameness was eye-opening for them. These men didn't just say, "We're allies!" They demonstrated their Ally Leadership by backing up their comments with action and donating millions of dollars to make change happen.

How Are Ally Leaders Made?

I often wonder why some people are true allies out of the gate and why others take years to grow into allies. I interviewed several of my colleagues, all fellow leaders who hold executive positions, and I asked them the question: When was the moment you decided to take action to become an Ally Leader?

Though their answers varied, they could all pinpoint the specific moment when their eyes were opened, their hearts were shifted, and they decided to take action. For a friend of mine who is a mega pastor, his shift happened suddenly. He shared how his wife and three daughters accompanied him to a conference in Australia, where he thought they would enjoy learning from various speakers on the topic of leadership. Unfortunately, he quickly became disappointed; they didn't see one female speaker onstage during the three-day conference. To his credit, he saw the discrepancy and realized that he had the power to do something about it, and do something about it he did. His church now has both men and women leading side by side and making an impact.

Here are a few other examples from leaders who recall what caused them to become an Ally Leader.

Three Profiles in Ally Leadership

I was the Senior Vice President of Marketing for Disney Channels Worldwide at The Walt Disney Company from 2015-2020. This was my last position during my proud fifteen years with Disney. Add to that ten years at Warner Bros., and you have an entertainment exec who has a whole lot of experience.

So, how did I personally take action as an Ally Leader in the workplace?

I am awfully proud to have embraced DEI before it was commonplace, i.e. before that fateful and fatal May 25, 2020. After the death of George Floyd, many corporations put their attention onto diversity initiatives. Some of them earnestly and proactively, but most of them performatively and reactively. And insincerely.

Many of us at Disney did diversity before we "had to." So, what did this "male, pale, stale, frail" executive possibly do to help this important movement?

1. **Be Open.** We advantaged types had a four-hundred-year head start. I realized it was well past time to give others the seats. Therefore, as an aging exec interested in paying it forward, I flagged this growing movement as an opportunity to be on the right side of history. And to be honest, I

was equally interested in leveraging all karma and executive attention possible, for my future professional benefit. I liked to zag when my peers zigged.

2. **Be Active.** I was as surprised as anyone to learn that I had been chosen as the executive sponsor of "The Bond," Disney's largest ERG (employee resource group), dedicated to the recognition, inclusion, and elevation of Black and African-American cast members. But they knew they had a well-connected and relatively fearless ally in me. So, I took action, just as you should. Take the call, take the meeting, sit through the debate, speak up and work through conflict, follow up and see that others got what they intended to get. Active.

3. **Be A Good Listener.** As the beneficiary of every conceivable double-standard in life, I knew I had no earthly idea what it was like to be on the short end of those demographic sticks. I told myself: *Let them teach me who they are, what they want, what success looks like to them, and how best to get there.*

4. **Be a Good Problem Solver.** One of our (many) "a-ha moments" was that, for all of the diversity in the candidate interviewee pool, if your interviewER pool was not equally diverse, "like" would keep hiring "like" and no measurable progress could be made in the makeup of our personpower. Once we ensured the right folks were on *both* sides of the interview desk, real, lasting employee/executive changes could begin occurring across the two-hundred thousand Disney employees.

If you are personally uncomfortable with any of the creative choices of your cherished Disney brand—casting, storytelling, re-casting—you should check yourself.

Ally Leadership only takes root when you are soberly self-aware about what your brand and your personpower do well, aware of what yet is still to be accomplished, then roll up your damn sleeves.

John Rood

As the Co-CEO of DMI Consulting, a multicultural strategic firm, and founder of the Alliance for Inclusive and Multicultural Marketing (AIMM), an industry-wide membership organization committed to representing the interests of diverse segments in the marketing/advertising industry, it's important that as an Ally Leader I practice what I preach.

This means that I value a diverse composition of staff/executives and strive to seek board members who mirror the diversity of our country. It means that I commit to listening and placing value on different perspectives before making a final decision. I attribute the growth of my company and the industry to those who are like me *and* unlike me, as diversity of ideas and experiences is what maximizes corporate escalation. Sadly, it's also what sometimes isolates people, keeps them far from their families, and makes it difficult for them to feel like they actually belong in a workforce and want to stay.

I understand that firsthand because I chose to move to the United States from Puerto Rico—where my family stayed—to pursue a career. I didn't have family near me, and I had to find friends who became my family over time. I spoke English fluently, but my cultural cues and expectations were quite different than those around me. So is the case for those in my office, where I employ people from other countries, cultures, races, generations, and identities. Because I understand the sacrifices they might make and the hardships they may face in order to have a successful career, I try to create an environment where they can celebrate who they are, and even go home more often than once a year for a couple of weeks of vacation.

At DMI, we've done this in a few ways: We have added Identity Day as a holiday that our employees can take any day of the year to celebrate who they are. We close our office at the end of the year so that *everybody* gets to spend the new year with family and friends, getting energized for the coming year. With the pandemic, we learned the importance of work/life balance, where life became a priority over work for so many, especially the younger people in our workforce. We've updated our office policies so our employees are able to work remotely from anywhere they want. Of course, we continue to have a hybrid model where people work half in the office and half at home.

As the job market continues to tighten, we have learned that benefits and compensation alone will not attract new talent to our company. Today's executives who are looking for new opportunities are exploring company culture first and foremost. Our message is one in which we embrace all, support all, and are not only open to differences but are also excited about having those differences in our workforce. It's not always easy having a diverse staff; it takes patience and commitment, but it's so worth it, personally and professionally.

Lisette Arsuaga

Before coming to the Global Leadership Network, I served for thirty-two years as the senior pastor of LCBC Church, a weekly community of more than 22,000 people whose lives have been, and continue to be, changed by Jesus Christ.

When it comes to leadership in the church and matters of faith, there is nothing that stirs emotions or invites stronger responses than when dealing with decisions about the best way to raise our children and keep them interested in God and faith.

I stepped head-first into that hornet's nest when one of my closest friends and strongest financial supporters approached me and informed me that as a parent of two pre-teenagers, he was not pleased with the staff member in charge of our high school ministry.

Now, I would be the first to acknowledge that this high school ministry leader did not fit the mold for leaders at LCBC Church. Although he is socially engaging, of high character and moral fabric, and has strong values of faith, he is also different than the other three-hundred people on our staff. This person is a little quirky, brilliant, and somewhat of an intellectual. After observing him and working alongside him for more than seven years, I believed in him as a leader. And, in this instance, I chose to be his ally.

Simply put, my friend did not feel that this person was a leader, nor did he believe his children would ever be able to relate to this person. Therefore, my friend advised me to fire this person and to move on to someone more suited (in his opinion) to student ministry.

Over numerous discussions, I shared with my friend this leader's past successes in ministry. I also described the leadership skills and strengths that I had observed in this leader over the years. And I acknowledged his differences and weaknesses. Then, I shared with my friend my decision to stand by this leader by keeping him on staff rather than releasing him, as my friend had strongly suggested.

Ultimately, my decision to stand by this leader did not come without great costs. Because I did not fire this leader, my friend and his family chose to leave our church. I was heartbroken. Out the door walked some of our strongest volunteer leaders, some of our strongest financial supporters (they had recently pledged to give their second million-dollar gift to our church), as well as one of my closest friends.

Yet, while I mourned the loss of my friendship, at the same time I found peace in the fact that I did not base this decision on peer or financial pressure, but rather I had chosen to be an ally to this person because of the merits of his leadership.

And now, years later, this leader continues to grow and excel in his leadership skills and has proven himself to be more than worthy to be a part of our team. As for my lost friend, sadly I must say that this relationship has yet to be mended.

As a leader, you will face criticism. That goes with the territory. And at times that criticism is not directed at you personally, but rather at those who serve with you. It is in those moments that you must decide what type of leader you will be. Will you be a leader who is an ally to others and stand up for your team members, or will you choose to shrink back and simply be thankful the criticism wasn't directed at you?

David Ashcraft

A friend of mine had an interesting take about this concept of how Ally Leaders are made. The CEO of a global company, he felt that it had something to do with the environment in which a person grows up. If you grew up playing sports or in the military, you tended to be exposed to people who were not like you, but who shared the same interest. Therefore, you got to know the person on a deeper level because you had similar experiences. That connection often allowed you opportunities to support each other in various ways, essentially, to have each other's back. In both sports and the military, having each other's back is a prerequisite. Having each other's back is often the difference between winning and losing, living or dying.

One of my favorite movies is *Remember the Titans* starring Denzel Washington. The movie is a true story about a high school football team that was integrated in 1971. The team got off to a rough start as they tried to blend teenage boys from various backgrounds. Through trial and error, the team finally learned to have each other's back, and they went on to have an undefeated season, winning their state championship. It was a wonderful example of how to take a diverse team, remove all the egos, and put the best talent in the best position for the team to win.

There's a reason why our military starts everyone off in boot camp and essentially strips them of everything. They take a group of people who are unlike each other, remove their egos, and put them in the best position to win. Although you cannot go to this extreme at your company, you can certainly find other ways to strengthen community within your organization, whether that is incorporating team-building exercises throughout your onboarding process or doing team outings on a regular basis. There are ample opportunities to put you and your team in a situation where everyone can leave their ego at the door, sincerely get to know each other, have fun, and win. Great team dynamics exist because everyone is aligned with the same mission, everyone knows their role, and the leader respects and fosters the uniqueness of each team member.

Hopefully, by now you are beginning to see a theme. You need to establish an environment where everyone's strengths are utilized like they are in sports or the military. This type of assessment requires your attention. You must observe your team to notice their gifts, talents, skills, and abilities. As a leader, your job is to make sure you have the best players on the team. If you want to be the best leader possible, you will need to create a diverse team, remove the egos, and put them in the best position to win. Remember, when your team wins, you win.

Seek Action, Not Applause

People often think of racial or gender discrimination in extreme forms, like: Klansmen walking around with sheets over their heads; obvious sexual predators waiting to pounce at any moment; or name-calling or violence directed at a male colleague who is openly gay. Most of us won't face those types of extremists, but we will face the daily subtle, covert discriminatory jabs that cause discrimination to remain pervasive in the workplace and within communities. For example, a black person being followed around a store by a salesperson; a woman being cut off mid-sentence in a meeting; or a brown person being mistaken for the help.

As an Ally Leader, when you see something, you have to say or do something. Witnessing racism, sexism, or bias and feeling badly about it doesn't change things. Taking action does.

As soon as the passenger approached the gate, I knew he was drunk. A gate agent for five years with Piedmont Airlines back in the 1990s, I had come face-to-face with a number of inebriated customers wanting to board an airplane. Policy stipulated that anyone who exhibited obvious behavior consistent with intoxication would not be allowed to board. So, when this customer, a middle-aged white man, stumbled to the counter wreaking of alcohol and handed me his crumpled boarding pass, I knew what I had to do.

"Sir, what city are you flying to today?" I asked in an effort to gauge just how snookered this guy was based on his speech.

He mumbled something that didn't sound like Atlantic City, the destination for this flight.

"Sir, how many drinks have you had today?" I continued, not expecting an honest answer, but giving this guy one more chance to prove me wrong.

That's when he became belligerent, and his already bloodshot eyes bulged with impatience.

"Why are you asking me these questions?" he said. "Just take my ticket and let me get to my seat. You didn't ask anyone else these stupid questions. What is this?"

With that, he began spewing a slew of curse words at me and demanding I move out of his way. With each word, his voice grew louder and louder.

Just then, Marie, another gate agent, ran over to assist me with what was becoming an increasingly hostile situation. There we stood, two black women trying to calm a drunken, irate passenger while the rest of the passengers at the gate nervously looked on. As Marie began to speak calmly to the man, he suddenly spouted the infamous N-word. As two adults, Marie and I had heard the word before, and this certainly (and unfortunately) wasn't the first time either of us had been called a nigger.

As the guy continued to cause a scene, our supervisor Gary arrived to help smooth the situation. Gary, a short, middle-aged white gentleman, had been our supervisor for years, and he knew the quality and professionalism of the work Marie and I produced. Gary was the type of leader who would jump in to assist the team whenever needed. He was an action-oriented leader who led by example.

Unaware of what had transpired, Gary asked the drunken passenger, "Sir, how can I help you?"

Without hesitation, the intoxicated passenger said eight words that would forever change how I viewed Gary: "These niggers won't let me board my flight."

A bit stunned by what he heard, Gary asked, "Excuse me; what did you say?"

Again, without hesitation, the customer pompously repeated, "These niggers won't let me board."

All of a sudden, Gary completely lost it. He snatched the ticket from the drunken passenger's hand and began to rip it to pieces. Then, at the top of his lungs, Gary screamed, "Who do you think you are? Don't you ever say that about these ladies! As a matter of fact, we don't want your kind flying onboard our aircraft. I will make sure that you are never allowed to fly on our airline again. You are not welcome here, so we will not be booking you on the next flight or any other flight for that matter. Now get out of here before I call security."

And with that, Gary threw the torn-up boarding pass back at the guy. In disbelief, Marie and I stood frozen. Gary's face was bright red, veins were popping out of his neck, and his eyes glared at the passenger like he wanted to burn a hole through his head. With that, the drunken man turned and stumbled away.

The remaining passengers in the boarding areas stood to their feet and gave Gary a thunderous round of applause, and Marie and I smothered Gary with the biggest hugs ever. That was Ally Leadership in action.

Rarely will you need to exhibit the type of fiery passion that Gary displayed, but you will need to take action in order to be an ally. You are not an ally just because you say you're an ally. You are only an ally when your head and heart, and your words and actions align.

One of the most interesting aspects of that situation wasn't the drunken passenger, and it wasn't even about Gary (although I am forever grateful for his Ally Leadership). The most interesting part of the situation for me was the other passengers in the boarding area who applauded Gary's actions. How many of them were disgusted by the comments and behavior of the drunk guy as they sat there listening to him spew obscenities and racial slurs, yet they did and said nothing? Of course, they didn't work for the airline, so perhaps they thought it best to be safe and merely observe as bystanders. What they demonstrated, however, was action-less observation, and in the end, that means nothing.

When you hear a colleague tell a raunchy, sexist, or racist joke or use a slur to describe another person or group and you say nothing, you earn *their* status rather than demonstrating your true allyship. You know that your colleague would never be brave enough to use that kind of language directly to the marginalized person. But somehow, they feel comfortable enough to say it to you. Why is that? Most likely it is because that colleague thinks you're like him. And that should disturb you enough to do something about it, to correct him. It takes courage to do so, and the rewards might not be seen by others, but the greatest reward is in you knowing that you have done something to correct a wrong even when you won't be acknowledged for it. The reward, in fact, is knowing that you win as an ally. That is Ally Leadership in action.

If you witness an unfairness happening to someone who is not like you and you do something or say something about it, you will make an impact and you will have exercised Ally Leadership. But don't get on your high horse and expect a pat on the back. Even as you practice Ally Leadership, the truth is that allies will not always be immediately welcomed or praised. Just because you say and (preferably) do Ally Leadership type of stuff, does not mean that people who are not like you will automatically trust your intentions. Most people proceed with caution in the face of the unfamiliar. This is where your authenticity needs to be exhibited.

When I coached executives, I would often tell them that they would need to do a complete 180-degree turn before their employees would give them even the slightest bit of credit for any change. Oftentimes, leaders will do a 360-degree assessment—a tool that helps people understand their strengths and weaknesses—and then set out to make significant changes based on the feedback. Periodically, when I would ask them how things were going, they would excitedly brag about how much they had changed. My response was always the same: "It doesn't matter how much *you* think you've changed. What matters is if *they* think you have changed."

It does not matter if *you* think you are an ally; it only matters if those you lead think you are an ally. Ally Leadership credit is given only to those who take action, and it is given by those you impact and influence; it's not a participation trophy you can award to yourself.

Performative vs. Authentic Ally Leadership

I like to think of performative Ally Leaders as people who are "all talk and no action" kind of people. You know the type. They are forever talking about how they believe in diversity, but they don't have any diversity on their leadership team or leadership pipeline. Or they proudly beat their chest stating they respect all cultures in the workplace, yet they ignore or deny observance of religious and cultural holidays recognized by their employees. Or my favorite, the ones who brag about how they have a wife and are proud "girl dads," yet they still have a pay gap the size of Texas between their male and female employees.

Performative "all talk no action" leaders are simply not needed. There's much to do when it comes to equality, and those who say they are allies but have absolutely no proof to back up their statements stand in the way of progress.

Paul Scanlon, author, podcast host, and leadership coach, shared a post on social media about how he showed his Ally Leadership by stopping a racial joke before it got started. Paul described a time when he was at a dinner party, and seated at his table were all white men. Paul is white as well. One of the men began to tell a joke and Paul could tell by how the joke was positioned that it was a racial joke. So, before the joke teller got too far into it, Paul interrupted him and politely said, "I don't think this joke is one I want to hear. I don't like where it's going. I think it is going to be at the expense of black people. I am uncomfortable with that. Do you mind not telling it? Or, I can leave the table." He went on to share that his statement caused an uneasiness at the table. This is an example of authentic Ally Leadership in action.

Without action, it's not Ally Leadership. Ally Leaders are people of bravery. They are people who are confident in their own abilities, who don't need to degrade others in order to make themselves feel powerful. Authentic Ally Leaders are already powerful. One could say that their courage comes from their confidence. Typically, Ally Leaders have had a great deal of success in their careers; that's why they are either in a leadership position or on a fast track to becoming a leader. Ally Leaders are learners, they know they do not know everything, and they believe school is never out for the pro. Ally Leaders read books like this because they want to be known as a great leader to everyone within their influence.

KEY TAKEAWAYS

- Reflecting on John, Lisette, or David's stories, what resonated with you most?
- Taking action as an Ally Leader can sometimes be uncomfortable. What one thing are you most afraid of?

TAKE ACTION

Decide how you're going to conquer the one thing you're most afraid of so you can take action as an Ally Leader.

WINNING IN THE WORKPLACE

WINNING IS SOMETHING LEADERS THINK about and do often. Your ability to win, and win often, is how you wound up in leadership. But as you venture into this new role as an Ally Leader, it may be worth visiting the science behind winning.

The secret to winning is . . . winning. It's called the Winning Effect. The more you win at something, the more your body captures those feelings and memories and the more dopamine—the chemical that makes you feel happy—your brain produces.

That feeling of winning shows up a lot for you as a leader. You feel it when your team wins a big contract, when you hit your numbers consistently, when your company is recognized in your industry, and even when you are right about . . . well, anything. Being right is akin to winning because it activates the same chemicals as winning. These dopamine-induced feelings of happiness, satisfaction, and relief can quickly become a feedback loop making your brain crave the feelings more. Because dopamine is produced in the same area of the brain that controls pleasure and rewards, you can become addicted to winning, if not careful.

Unfortunately, some leaders can become so focused on being right that they can't even consider other people's views and realities. My mentor, the late Judith E. Glaser, explains in her 2013 *Harvard Business Review* article, "Your Brain Is Hooked on Being Right," that the addiction to being right is a neurochemical process. When you argue and win, your brain gets flooded with adrenaline and dopamine which makes you feel good, dominant, and invincible. In a tense meeting, you will look to replicate those feelings, which can cause an addiction to being right.

You were probably somewhat addicted to winning or being right early in your career. You were large and in charge. You felt like you knew it all . . . until you didn't. As you grew in your leadership, you quickly humbled yourself, or you were humbled by your mistakes, and you learned that you don't know everything, nor do you need to. One of the problems with winning often, and becoming addicted to it, is that winning isn't sustainable. At some point, you're going to lose or mess up or get it wrong. Leaders who don't yet know what that feels like tend to think they are always right and that everyone will always go along with their way of doing things. In reality, life just doesn't work that way.

The best leaders know that they don't know everything, and they work extra hard to surround themselves with people who know more than they do. The best leaders also know that growing in their knowledge is a walk that never ends. As an Ally Leader, one of the best ways to extend your winning streak without becoming a pompous know-it-all is to understand that you win whenever you help others win.

The science of winning explains that your body produces the same chemical reaction to seeing someone else win as if you have won, assuming you wanted them to win in the first place. This is especially true in sports. Ever attend a sporting event where you were surrounded by hundreds of people you didn't know? Then suddenly, your team scores a goal, the stadium breaks into a roar, people cheer at the top of their lungs and high-five each other. That mixture of giddiness and elation is your dopamine going through the roof. Although you didn't personally score the goal or have anything to do with winning the game, your body chemically responds as if you did. (The same can happen if you're watching the game at home alone.)

The good news is that there is another chemical that feels just as good as adrenaline, and that is oxytocin. Activated by human connection, oxytocin opens up the networks in your brain that allow for sharing. As an Ally Leader, one way that you can activate oxytocin in yourself and others is to shift your mindset from a position of having to know everything and always being right, to one of curiosity and learning from others, thereby positioning you as a leader who demonstrates that learning from others and winning go hand in hand.

Diversity, Equity, Inclusion, and Belonging: What They Really Mean

Many companies have had diversity departments for decades. Back in the day, they were sometimes known as the department of affirmative action, which later morphed into the equal opportunity department, and then the diversity department. The equity, inclusion, and belonging additions grew from the need to expand the way companies and organizations viewed, hired, promoted, advanced, and listened to individuals who represented groups that had been marginalized for far too long. Even still, some leaders struggle to grasp a true understanding of these concepts.

Here is how I explain DEIB. Let's say you hire a female executive and she is the first female to join the leadership team. *Diversity* means that now that you have a female on board, your team is considered diverse. You can now check that box. *Equity* means that this new female executive will receive equal pay for equal work. You can now check that box. *Inclusion* means that the rest of the leadership team welcomes her and outlines for her how things are done around here, so she can fit in and adapt to the current structure. You can now check that box. *Belonging* means that the leadership team welcomes her and together, the entire team—not just her—makes adjustments because her presence has and will change the dynamics of the group. Do you see the difference?

Understand what diversity, equity, inclusion, and belonging is and is not. The problem is that many companies and leaders don't authentically understand DEI; therefore, they make DEI initiatives to be performative rather than authentic. As with all performative measures, if not implemented correctly, they can easily build resentment. One of the reasons people keep talking about diversity subjects such as DEIB is because there seems to be a lot of talk but little movement. Some people suggest that white male leaders are the catalysts who could dramatically help to speed things up in this area, likely because white men are typically the ones holding the power and leadership positions in the workplace. But Houston, we have a problem. Research also shows that white men are feeling left out of the DEI movement.

In a 2022 *Forbes* article titled, "White Men Are Feeling Left Out of DEI; Why Should We Care and What Should We Do?" writer Teresa Hopke states that 70% of white men feel uncertain whether DEI includes them, causing them to either disengage or not commit to it at all. How interesting that a movement about including everyone has some feeling excluded. The article goes on to say that many white men feel that women and minorities are being given preference over them and that they just want everything to be fair. However, this thought process only works if you believe everything was fair all along.

If you had a pie and one group historically received a larger portion of the pie, that means the remaining groups received a smaller portion. If you're trying to even things out, then the group that historically received a larger portion is going to get less than what they're used to. In the end, they're getting their fair share. Much of this can be resolved by including white men into the inclusion process.

As a leader, your goal should not be to check the DEIB box. Instead, your objective is to create a culture where everyone is seen, appreciated, and feels psychologically safe, where their unique perspectives are valued and encouraged. DEI initiatives in corporate America tend to move slowly, if at all, because many companies are doing performative DEIB, which can be exhausting. Companies might establish and achieve diverse hiring quotas (check that box), but they don't make systemic adjustments that incorporate fair hiring, compensation, and advancement practices into the fabric of the company.

DEIB should be approached as individual pillars because each pillar plays a support role in helping the business attract and retain top talent and diversify its thought patterns to remain competitive in the areas of product, pricing, and process. A diverse team adds depth to a company's brainpower because of their varying backgrounds and lived experience. A team where everyone is paid, developed, and expected to perform at a high level is good for creating top producers. And top producers perform best when they feel like they belong. Diversity, equity, inclusion, and belonging are each incredibly different and warrant different actions and outcomes.

Diversity

To have a competitive advantage, you need a diverse team of people who think and see things differently from each other and whose communication styles and problem-solving capabilities differ. Because the world is so interconnected, having a global viewpoint is not just the right thing to do, it's the smart thing to do.

The rate at which diverse teams out-produce non-diverse teams is staggering. Racially diverse teams are 35% more likely to outperform their less diverse counterparts, according to *McKinsey & Company's* December 2023 report titled, "Diversity Matters Even More: The Case for Holistic Impact." For every 10% increase in racial and ethnic diversity on the senior executive team, earnings before interest and taxes (EBIT) rise 0.8%. From a gender perspective, companies that have more women in executive roles are 25% more likely to outperform their counterparts.

In other research, *Forbes* contributor Erik Larson writes in his 2017 article, "New Research: Diversity + Inclusion = Better Decision Making At Work," that diverse teams deliver 60% better results and make better decisions in 87% of cases.

In a September 2023 article in *World Economic Forum* titled "4 Ways Companies Can Make Real Progress on DEI," authors Elisabeth Pipic and Silja Baller state that companies should implement a whole business approach when it comes to DEI efforts. Linking policy development, employee engagement, technology, learning, communications, and multi-stakeholder collaboration to DEI objectives embeds them as an integral part of the core business mandate.

As an example, a company can add DEI benchmarks for each department, not just for hiring and recruitment. For the finance department, you could include a metric to diversify your suppliers. For the sales and marketing teams you could measure market expansion via diversification, for customer service teams, you could do a language audit to determine how many languages your service reps speak, thereby allowing you to serve more customers. And for operations, you could review your overall service experiences to ensure that all clients feel like they are welcomed.

At one of the aviation companies I worked for, we had to take a hard look at ourselves and realize that we were not living up to our expectations. Our customer service reps only spoke English even though we were global, our onboard amenities did not take into account the needs of women, our marketing material had no diverse images, our sales team had no diverse employees, we had no diverse suppliers, the list goes on and on. And yet, we proudly proclaimed we were champions of diversity. Really? One by one, we began to chip away at each of these items. The results were amazing! Within eighteen months we had increased the number of diverse clients by more than 200 percent, which added tens of millions of dollars in sales to the company.

I had just read the paper and was literally jumping up and down in my kitchen with excitement. A super talented friend of mine was just announced as a new officer for one of the Fortune 500 companies. She was going to be their first black C-suite executive. This was huge for her and us as black women! I know firsthand what it's like to be one of the few black C-suite executives for a publicly held company. It is historic and it also carries a heavy weight. I wanted her to know that she had my support, so I called her a few months later, after she'd had time to settle in.

She confided that she was still adjusting. "Listen," I said, "I know, the struggle is real, I get it. What can I do to help?"

I wanted to offer my support because she and so many other black female executives were there for me when the announcement came out that I had made history as America's first black president of a major private jet company. Many black female executives sent me private notes saying, "You are changing the face of corporate America. We're proud of you. Tell us how we can help." The least I could do was to repay the favor, and it was my honor to do so.

My friend shared that she was trying to soak up as much information as she could. This was a new industry for her, so she was knee-deep in learning. The executive team she joined had been working together for years, so not only was she new to the industry, but she was also the newbie on the team. She shared that one day, her boss pulled her aside to check in and see how she was adapting to her new role. He mentioned that he noticed that she was quiet during the meetings, and he probed to understand why.

He was empathetic to the fact that besides her, everyone else on the team had been together for years and information was flowing back and forth rather quickly due to the team's familiarity with each other. He suggested that if ever she didn't understand something, she should feel free to pull him aside and ask whatever questions she needed to. He extended an offer to mentor her on the side if she felt it would help. She was appreciative of the gesture. She then confided in him that she would need time to make some mental shifts. She explained that as a woman, and especially as a woman of color, we are often hesitant to share when we don't know something because that lack of knowledge is often weaponized against us.

The structure of corporate America hasn't always welcomed people who are not white and male. Even for Ally Leaders who take action to welcome others, they have to understand that fitting in isn't always easy. That isn't the "problem" of the other people; it is a reality of the system, tradition, and history. As an Ally Leader, you must be aware of this, be patient, provide resources and support, and allow people to navigate the system as they find their way in it.

In particular, if you are a male Ally Leader, pay close attention to this. It is imperative that you know the burdens that your female and/or minority colleagues carry. The standards to which we are held are higher than most. As a black female, I know that if I make a mistake it won't be a reflection on me alone; it will be viewed as a judgment against all potential black female executives. That's a heavy burden to bear. Leaders who are male and white don't carry that same burden. If they make a mistake, it's just a mistake; it's not a condemnation against an entire gender or race.

Equity

Within the DEI equation, leaders can sometimes get lost on the "E" portion. In its simplest form, equity is an acknowledgment that we don't all start from the same place. Adjustments are often needed to balance things out.

Take the US Women's National Soccer team as an example. In 2016, the team sued the US Soccer Federation for gender discrimination primarily focused on pay inequity. The women's soccer team had won more games than the men's team, their matches generated more revenue than the men's did, and yet they were making less money than their male counterparts. This was a perfect example of a systematic disparity.

It turns out that our brain is disgusted by unfairness. A September 29, 2020 article on Medium.com titled "Why unfairness makes you rage" written by Dana G. Smith reveals that there is an area in your brain called anterior insula which gets activated when you perceive unfairness. This same area is also involved in feelings of empathy and disgust, suggesting that you are literally repulsed by inequality. The amygdala also gets in on the action by triggering feelings of anger when you see or feel inequality. This might help explain why the US Men's National Soccer team stood in allyship with the Women's team to help emphasize the need for equal pay for their female counterparts. Fortunately, the women's team eventually won their suit.

Think about how this translates to you as an Ally Leader. Where are these areas of inequity within your team or company? Balancing out equity is low-hanging fruit for an Ally Leader—essentially, one of the easiest areas to address—and the lowest of fruit to pluck is pay equity. Does everyone who does the same job and has the same work experience start off making the same amount on your team? If not, why not? Dig into the details of this and then ask yourself one question: If I had to stand in front of a judge or the proverbial moral police, could I give solid justification backed by facts and data as to why there is a disparity? If you can, great. If you cannot, then you now have a wonderful opportunity to exercise your Ally Leader muscles.

Inclusion

Ahhh, yes. I have twenty minutes before my next client call. That was enough time to gobble down my lunch and take a potty break. My schedule was tight, and I loved every minute of it.

In the summer of 2017, I was running my own coaching and consulting practice that specialized in communication skills for C-Suite executives and increased revenue generation for high-ticket sales professionals. By then, I was retired from the aviation industry after twenty years, and consulting had become a seamless transition for me. Throughout my many years in business, I saw two needs that I felt my practice could address: leadership and communication. I have a heart for leaders because I know the job is hard. I also know that if you are an executive who doesn't know how to communicate, your job will be much harder. Leadership can be a lonely place, and being a subpar-communicator makes it even lonelier.

Coaching executives afforded me the opportunity to become their trusted advisor, to be a listening ear, and to be their biggest cheerleader as they tackled the tough stuff. For sales professionals, especially those who have an annual quota of $10MM+, the pressure to perform can be enormous. Being a salesperson is a noble profession. You spend your day trying to help people solve their biggest problems. Problems that, if solved, help make people's jobs and life easier. Oftentimes, I found that salespeople who sold big dollar amounts simply needed help learning how to be more efficient with their time and more effective with their message.

I absolutely loved my job and my clients. Every day I wanted to pinch myself because I got paid to work with winners, people who were incredibly smart and who wanted to make a difference in the world. They were focused on accelerating the people and profits of their businesses.

Halfway through my sandwich, the phone rang. I could see that it was a CEO client of mine. Whenever a client called me during a time that wasn't their scheduled appointment, I knew something was awry. When I answered, I could tell that he was rip-roaring mad. Placing my sandwich down, I redirected all of my attention to him.

"Hey, what's going on? You sound upset."

"She left!" he said.

"Who left?

Through exasperated breathing, he explained that his female CFO had stormed out of the office upset. She was angry because she had not been invited to go golfing with the rest of the leadership team, all men. My client was furious. I patiently listened to his fiery rant about how he viewed his CFO's behavior to be childish and overly sensitive. I allowed him ample time to unload all of his pent-up frustrations. I learned early on that sometimes the best thing to do when coaching high achievers is to give them space to unload. Being a leader is a tough job. People expect something from you at all times. As their trusted confidante, sometimes the best thing I could do for them was to just let them be—be mad, hurt, frustrated, scared, vulnerable, and even pissed. Just Be.

As he started to wind down and his words became few and far between, it seemed as if he had gotten it all off his chest. With the coast now clear, I asked him two simple questions.

"Why didn't you invite her to go golfing?"

Annoyed by my question, he flippantly answered, "Because she doesn't play golf."

My second question: "How would you feel if your board invited your entire executive team to go on an outing, but they didn't invite you? How would you feel?"

Silence. I could tell by the long, awkward pause that he was beginning to get it. After speaking with the CFO, she confirmed my suspicions. The issue wasn't that she didn't play golf; the issue, from her perspective, was that she wasn't even invited. She may have declined the offer, but she was never given that chance because she wasn't even asked.

When you think of the golf event as a simple golf game amongst peers, it doesn't seem like a big deal. However, when you think of a golf game in its totality, then it becomes a big deal. The female executive already knew what the men knew, that there are lots of deals being discussed on the golf course, projects that are reviewed, relationships that are cultivated, introductions to key people that can be arranged, and so forth. The golf game itself is not just a game, it's a time for business in a relaxed setting where critical conversations and relationships are cultivated.

When anyone who is equally pivotal to those conversations and decisions is not invited to participate, those opportunities are limited or eliminated, thereby leaving that person at a disadvantage. Often, that disadvantage prevents their upward mobility and fair opportunity to participate on other levels. If many of the conversations and decisions are happening on the proverbial golf course, and women (or others in an out-group) aren't present, then how well are their gifts being utilized? What can you do to ensure that everyone's gifts and talents are being maximized, applied, or at least considered?

Excluding women, in particular, might work in ministry (well, not really), but it is a terribly isolating and counter-productive method in the marketplace. In ministry, the concept behind the Modesto Manifesto, or what some call the "Billy Graham Rule," suggests that a pastor should never be alone with a woman without another person present, for the sake of how it may appear to others. While the idea might be considered a respectful way to protect the reputation of a minister or counselor from unfair accusations, this doesn't work in business.

Women are an essential part of the workforce in the 21st century; there's just no way around it (thankfully). Excluding women from what was once considered "The Old Boys Network" just doesn't cut it these days. Consider how that exclusion impacts a female leader. What opportunities is she not exposed to because she's not in the room? If she is not in the room, her talents are not there either. How might unused talents impact your company, church, community, or mandate? Here are some facts to consider:

- The 32 S&P 500 companies that have women CEOs significantly outperform companies run by men—in revenue, product sales, and profits combined (over the past ten years, the difference in returns is 384% from female-led versus 261% from male led).[2]

- The presence of women in managerial positions increases profits by 3% to 20%.[3]

- Gender-diverse executive teams are 21% more likely to experience above average profitability.

- 56.8% of gender-diverse executive teams report an increased ability to attract and retain talent.

- 60.2% of gender-diverse executive teams report increased profits year over year.

- 54.1% of gender-diverse companies report enhanced company reputation among industry experts and their customer base.[4]

---

[2] "Are Female CEOs better than male CEOs?" Personal Finance Club, March 7, 2023 (Updated March 18, 2024). https://www.personalfinanceclub.com/are-female-ceos-better-than-male-ceos/

[3] Esade, "Women's Leadership: A major competitive advantage," Do Better, June 15, 2023. https://dobetter.esade.edu/en/women-leadership-competitive advantage#:~:text=Benefits%20of%20women's%20leadership&text=They%20show%20greater%20innovation%20and,and%20attract%20talent%20more%20effectively.

[4] Kara Denison, "Businesses Succeed with Women in Leadership: It's Time to Make the Workplace More equitable for Women," Forbes, December 15, 2022. https://www.forbes.com/sites/karadennison/2022/12/15/businesses-succeed-with-women-in-leadership-its-time-to-make-the-workplace-more-equitable-for-women/?sh=510aaa601aa8

As an Ally Leader, you want to lead diverse teams, not because it's the right thing to do, but also because it's just smart business and you are a smart business leader.

By 1993, we had been living in Florida for a few years, and I was finally getting settled into my new job as a corporate sales manager in the travel and hospitality industry after having packed up my family and moving from Connecticut. The company's CEO invited me to join his new team and had even created a position just for me. Excited to do something different, I plunged into my work full steam ahead. That first year, I traveled and was gone from my family 270 days. By year two, I was completely burnt out and left the job.

Needing to reset and reprioritize family life, we joined our local church, which was made up of mostly young families like us. With my life much more balanced, I now had time to volunteer and serve in several ministries. My favorite was the women's ministry. I had a particular interest in enhancing the development opportunities of our female churchgoers. The church leaders saw my passion and eventually bought into my vision of what the horizon could look like for our female congregants.

It was 10 a.m. one Saturday morning and I had come to the church to meet with the pastoral team to discuss the upcoming women's event. The conference room door was shut, and I could hear voices, which meant that another meeting was still underway.

As I stood in the hallway patiently waiting, the pastor's assistant came over and said, "Hey, Steph, sorry this meeting is still going on and is now eating into your meeting time. They should be done in fifteen minutes. Pastor wanted me to have you come into the board room so you're not out here standing in the hallway by yourself."

"Sounds good," I said. "Thank you."

As I followed her into the room with the meeting still in progress, I was mindful not to distract from what was being discussed. Quietly, I made eye contact with everyone in the room, shot them a quick smile, and took my seat. I sat listening to all the leaders share their ideas on how best to do outreach and invite visitors to the church. In the midst of it, I couldn't help but think, *Wow, these are some really bad ideas.* I saw church outreach like new business development, and as a person who specialized in new business development, I struggled with the ideas that were being tossed around. But since this wasn't my meeting and I wasn't on the leadership team, I decided to hold my tongue.

As the meeting progressed and the bad ideas kept flowing in like the world's greatest hits, I couldn't contain myself any longer. I blurted out a few questions that seemed to stop everyone in their tracks. Silence. Feeling the stares from the meeting attendees, I decided to not push my fate any further with more questions. Instead, I sat back in my chair and kept my mouth shut for the remainder of the meeting.

To my pastor's credit, after the meeting, he pulled me aside and said, "Stephanie, I sensed that you had more to say but that you held back. Is that correct?"

"Yes, you're right," I replied. "I got the feeling from the others that it wasn't my place to question the ideas that were being presented, so I stopped."

Thank goodness my pastor wasn't stacked with pride, but instead exercised wisdom. He then said, "Stephanie, I'd like to hear your ideas and what you were going to say. I know that your work outside the church was in business development, and I think since you grew markets for a living, you could provide a unique perspective that those of us in ministry may not have. Let's discuss your ideas."

The pastor demonstrated Ally Leadership that day because he asked, listened, and learned about my ideas, then he took action. It didn't matter to him that I was a woman and not on the leadership team. He knew my area of expertise and he welcomed my input. He knew the value of hearing from those who are not like him, and how pivotal those voices could be to the success of the church.

I often find that newer or more junior employees can often provide the best insight because they don't usually know the history of "how things are done around here." That alone can be a blessing. Creating an environment where ideas go to blossom versus die on the vine is essential to being a good Ally Leader.

Belonging

Fitting in isn't always easy initially. Whether the rookie is the newest member on your executive team who happens to be Korean, the first openly LGBTQ+ member of your staff, or the first Hispanic man to lead your HR department, the problem isn't them as the rookie, the newbie, the first, or the only. The problem is a reality of the system, tradition, and history that has brought you and your company to an inflection point. There, you can face the opportunity to thrive in the 21st-century workplace.

As an Ally Leader, you have to be aware of some of the challenges your employees face as they attempt to belong—not to be confused with assimilate. Make it clear that no one has to change who they are as a person in order to fit into your in-group. Yes, there are policies about workplace behavior, productivity, teamwork, and communication that need to be adhered to; however, when it comes to appearance don't assume that they can't do the job because they don't fit your definition of "normal." If they have tattoos or their hair is bald, braided, or bright green—don't let that deter you from asking, listening, and learning about them (and their form of self-expression).

Be patient, provide resources and support, and allow people to navigate as they find their way in the new space. If you need help understanding their experience and perspective, be sure to ask, listen, and learn. It's a lot for an Ally Leader to contend with, but when you approach it as an opportunity to learn and improve, the burden goes away.

Some indications that your diverse hires are not getting the support they need to be their best in the workplace include:

- They exit sooner than other new hires.
- They do not participate regularly in group engagements (meetings, brainstorming, etc.).
- They simply don't exist on your team.

These behaviors indicate that you might be missing a key ingredient in the DEIB equation—the "B". People just don't feel like they belong, and that's a problem you must address. When you notice these things, you need to check your systems. Does your current system allow people to be themselves, or do the powers that be require them to emulate someone else?

Can they exercise self expression? For an example: If the required attire is a suit, can they wear any colored suit that they'd like—or does it have to be a dark blue suit?

Can they decide how they get their job done, or do they have to do it exactly like everyone else?

Can they be creative and think outside the norm, or is that not encouraged?

If you are unsure how to answer that question, here are some actions you can take.

- Review your current systems (HR policies, hiring, training, mentorship, promotion, reviews, etc.) and make sure there's no bias within the policies.
- Get input from every level of the company or organization.
- Get input and buy-in from various groups represented within the company (genders, ethnicities, religious backgrounds, physical abilities, etc.).

- Make adjustments regularly (bi-annually is ideal).
- Ask for feedback to determine what's working and what's not working.

Systems that support DEIB make adjustments as new people are welcomed in. This might sound like a lot of change for your organization, and it is. Consider how much change your new hires or newly promoted coworkers experience when fitting into a system that was not created for them to succeed, nor is designed to be welcoming for them as they progress. Successful efforts to create an environment of belonging rely on ensuring that every level of leadership is keenly aware of the diversity of their own department, that they have a strategy to attract and retain top diverse talent, and that they consciously and intentionally create space to welcome new people and ensure they have equal access and are treated fairly so they feel they belong.

Ally Leaders See the Big Picture

Ally Leadership spans the gamut in the workplace and includes not only your engagement with people from a different race, culture, religion, or gender classification than you, but also includes those in different departments within the company.

One of the most professional scoldings I have ever received involved departmental Ally Leadership. It was one of those days that was jammed-packed with chaos; a day that seemingly would never end. By 3 p.m. I had been going so long and so fast that I felt like it was midnight. It seemed like everything that could go wrong that day did. Deals were either going sideways, getting postponed, or simply not closing. As a sales leader, this was my day from hell.

As I stood in the break room staring at the Keurig machine waiting for what seemed like my one-hundredth cup of coffee to finish brewing, my CEO popped in. Based on his chipper, light-hearted attitude, it was clear that his day was going far better than mine.

"Hey, Steph, how's your day going?" he asked.

As I proceeded to explain how my day was unfolding, I could tell he was listening and was empathetic.

When I finished, he randomly asked, "How are the pilots doing?"

Now, to be blunt, as the head of sales I didn't know or care how the pilots were doing that day because I was up to my eyeballs in my team's sales deals going off the rails. Confused by his question, and thinking he must have had a mental lapse and forgot that I was leading sales not operations, I asked for clarification.

"What do you mean, how are the pilots doing?"

He replied, "What do you mean, what do I mean? What are today's operational stats? How many aircraft are flying today? How many are down for maintenance? Any pilots call out today?"

At this point in the conversation, a million thoughts raced through my head: *What? How do I know? Why are you asking me about operations? I don't oversee that team. Did you not just hear me tell you about the deals that are going sideways? That's where my focus is.*

Instead, I simply replied, "I'm not sure, but I'm happy to go ask." I will never forget the look on his face as we stood glaring at each other for a solid minute, both of us confused by the other.

Finally, he said, "Aren't you the VP of sales? Don't the happenings in operations impact your sales team? If planes are down for maintenance or pilots are out sick, doesn't that impact our customers' experience, thus impacting your sales? How do you not know?"

And with that, I got schooled on departmental Ally Leadership.

After that subtle tongue lashing, I went downstairs to the operations center, sat down across the desk from the vice president of operations, and proceeded to have a lengthy conversation about everything that was currently going on with the pilots and operations. It was the most time I had ever spent discussing operations outside of an executive team meeting. I gained a detailed understanding of what challenges my colleague was dealing with, and learned of things my team and I could do to help lessen their burden.

The interaction with my CEO forever changed how I function as an executive. It caused me to elevate my focus from looking only at my own department to viewing the integration of each department of the company. Although I knew and respected the fact that each department had its own unique and necessary function, I quickly began to see the overlap in our work on the outcomes experienced overall.

Departmental Ally Leadership overlaps with Ally Leadership. Think about the different people and personalities within each department. Salespeople are usually very different than finance people, and folks in finance tend to be very different than those in marketing, and marketing people tend to be fundamentally different than those in operations. Once you add the virtual workforce into the equation, you can quickly see that Ally Leaders are constantly evolving to keep up with the needs of today's changing workforce.

The job of an Ally Leader is never done. There is always growth and room for improvement. It is our ability to evolve that helps us be excellent. Ally Leadership never stops.

How To Take the Initiative

By now, you know that being an effective Ally Leader requires you to take action. You have to make the effort to understand people who are not like you as well as people in other departments within your company. As a leader, you are used to stepping out first, doing what's needed, and going the extra mile. This is your time to use those skills to strengthen your ability and insights as an Ally Leader.

Below are some ways to help you do that. Don't worry; none of this is hard, but it does take some time and effort. You don't have to do it all in one go. But make the commitment to take at least one of these actions each week and see how it works for you. Remember, you don't get to be an Ally Leader by deciding it for yourself. You earn the Ally Leader title when others witness you demonstrating your new leadership actions.

- **Educate yourself.** Visit local culture museums and galleries. Oftentimes within various communities there are shops, galleries, and museums that display the history of that culture or community.

- **Communicate with your inner circle.** Let them know about your commitment to expand your understanding of people not like you. This conversation not only gives your circle a *heads up* on your intentions, but it will also shed light on their heart issues as well. Observe how they respond when you have that conversation. Are they supportive, or do they try to deter you from it? If they try to deter you from expanding your mind, you may want to consider the company you keep. If, on the other hand, they admire your courage and are supportive of it, then you can invite them along on your journey. As you build trusting relationships with people unlike you (your out-group), feel free to invite them to meet your other friends (your in-group). Together, you can make the unfamiliar familiar.

- **Go on social media.** Find a topic of interest, and then follow a creator or influencer who doesn't look like you who is an expert in that subject. Support their work.

- **Observe.** Spend this week observing every meeting you're in. Are there people in the meeting who don't look like you? Do they speak up in the meeting? When they speak up, how do people respond to them? How do *you* respond to them? If you find that a majority of your meetings consist of people who look and/or think like you, then think through how you can change that in the future. This could be as simple as inviting people who are not traditionally invited or who do not typically speak up in the meeting.

Keep in mind, if you do invite people who aren't traditionally invited, you will have to be proactive about preparing them and getting them to speak up within the meeting since this will be a new environment for them. Be mindful of the power dynamics. You could even meet with them beforehand to let them know that you admire their work and that you are inviting them to the meeting because you would like their input on what's being discussed.

- **Assess.** Take an assessment of your team(s). Is everyone on the team like you? If so, talk to HR about it. Coming from the private jet industry I've had to deal with this issue numerous times. Every team that I've inherited looked the same. They were all white men. It takes time to change a system. You may need to build a pipeline of diverse talent to ensure long-term results. In the short term, look at open positions within your department and insist that HR bring you qualified diverse candidates to interview. If you don't require, request, or insist on this, it won't happen.

As an effective Ally Leader, it is your responsibility to communicate your commitment to exploring and inviting a diverse slate of qualified candidates. Depending on the strength of your HR team, this may or may not be well received. Oftentimes, I have found that HR teams would rather take the path of least resistance by doing what they've always done. Typically, since they're trying to fill many positions, not just those in your department, they want to fill the positions and move on to the next one. Doing things differently will require extra effort on their part. They will need to think outside the box. Be prepared to push back on any excuses they may create. The most frequent one being, "There is no diverse talent out there."

Being a black female executive in the private aviation industry was groundbreaking, for sure. I was proud of my accomplishment, and grateful to lead a team of professionals who respected me. But I wasn't satisfied being the only black person on the team. So, when time came to hire new people, I wanted to make sure the pool of candidates was diverse.

When I strolled into the HR department to let them know of my desire to diversify my team, I was shocked at the response.

"I love my current team," I said, "but I want to see people who look different, think differently, and communicate differently."

With a blank look on her face, the HR director said, "Oh, yeah, Stephanie, we would love to diversify the team, but there is just no diverse talent out there in the industry."

What? That doesn't even sound right. I decided to play along with the charade to make it a teachable moment, so I rephrased her response and said, "So, you're telling me that in this multi-billion-dollar industry, that has over one hundred million people working in it, that there are no other women or people of color other than myself?"

Not only was the statement incorrect, it also showed a laziness (or maybe craziness, I'm not sure) on her part.

"Tell me about how your conversations went with Women In Aviation," I continued, "or the Organization of Black Aerospace Professionals or the National Gay Pilots Associations or the Latino Pilots Association or the Asian Pilots Association? I'm sure you've contacted them, so how did those conversations go?"

Crickets! The HR team had never reached out or even heard of those associations, which combined had more than one hundred-thousand members.

Gaining the diversity I wanted on my team required me to challenge the HR team and others to think outside the box and do something different. My goal was to get the most qualified candidates in front of me so I could hire the best talent. I wasn't looking to change the rules or the qualifications for the positions. I didn't want a sub-par employee in a position. What I wanted was a diverse team that would bring a diversity of perspectives. And I knew I could get it. You can too; you just have to take the initiative and insist your HR department makes the effort to find qualified candidates.

Besides diversifying your interviewees, be sure to also diversify your interviewers. Remember, diverse thinkers will have different perspectives. Therefore, they will ask different questions during the interview process, respond to questions differently, and explore opportunities through a different lens. Once you begin to have a more diverse team, be diligent to constantly review your processes and procedures to make sure you are not forcing your diverse employees to assimilate into a system that was not created with them in mind.

As you establish trusting relationships with people not like you, be sure to ask for feedback on your conduct. This might sound scary but trust me on this. When people see you making a sincere effort to be an ally, they take note.

In the summer of 2010, my company had just signed a brand partnership with a Korean airline to cross-promote our services. I was excited to be part of the launch team. Determined to deliver a compelling cross-cultural campaign and to show true allyship, our marketing team did a phenomenal job training everyone on various

Korean business etiquettes. We learned how to respect the chain of command when speaking to the leaders versus their staff, how to hand someone your business card using two hands, when to bow versus shake hands, and other appropriate gestures.

Unfortunately, the marketing team was so busy training on the etiquette protocols, they failed to research the marketing protocols. Instead, they went off by themselves and created these elaborate multi-million-dollar marketing campaigns that they were confident would impress our Korean counterparts. The problem was that they never asked our counterparts, or anyone of Korean descent, for feedback along the way. The campaign launched and it was a disaster. In the words of one of our Korean counterparts, the material "looked like we just wished death upon their families." Whoa!

How did this happen? We did what so many people do when it comes to allyship—we dove in head-first and didn't ask for feedback. We looked at things only through our lens because we thought we knew best. Had we asked, listened, and learned we would have discovered, prior to spending a million dollars, that although the color red was a dominant color within our brand and represented valor, energy, and passion, that same color in Korean screamed exorcism and reminded people of communism. Needless to say, the collateral was destroyed along with the marketing team's allyship ego.

When you sincerely wish to improve, make an impact, or win, you need to ask for honest feedback from people who represent those you are trying to impact. If you are not part of that group, you will miss the mark because you will view everything from your perspective, which is absent of the lived experience.

Try this simple approach to getting feedback on your Ally Leadership actions:

1. Take authentic action. Avoid seeking recognition for doing so.

2. Privately ask a trusted colleague who has witnessed your action for their feedback. Questions such as: What is one thing you would like to see me do more of to be a better ally? Are there any words I use that can be discriminatory? What one thing should I stop doing if I want to be a better Ally Leader?

3. Listen to their response.

4. Ask more clarifying questions.

5. Thank them for their input. Acknowledge the feedback as a gift and respond with a simple, "Thank you. I believe you."

6. Learn from the exchange. Make the proper adjustments, move on, and strive to improve.

THE WAY FORWARD

I T'S MARCH 2020, A GLOBAL pandemic has shut down the world, and I have multi-million-dollar assets sitting on the tarmac—my company's jets. In a matter of days, the skies have emptied as air traffic plummeted 94 percent worldwide and tens of millions of jobs are at risk, including my employees' . . . and my own.

I'm the president of a private aviation company, and I have to make some tough decisions. While our employees are hunkering down at home, trying to figure out how their family will manage school and work, wiping down mail and vegetables, and deciding whether to mask up or not, five C-suite executives from competing aviation companies meet every Sunday night via Zoom to figure out how to run the industry with no private jets in the sky. While our employees spend their days and nights re-evaluating their relationship to work—and to their leaders—my experience is entirely different. I am a leader, and I'm scrambling to help save our company and an entire industry. We're all making it up as we go along because no one has ever lived through or led through a pandemic.

By now, the world is on lockdown. Even if we *could* fly, nobody wants to go anywhere. Conferences are canceled. Vacations, canceled. Corporate travel, canceled. People are home, learning to make sourdough bread and reacquainting themselves with their loved ones on a full-time basis. They are also re-evaluating everything they believe about their relationship to work, asking the big questions about the meaning of life and work, and thinking differently about how they spend their time on earth.

When the crisis was over, the rules of work had changed, evolving into what *Forbes* called, "a strange new workplace" and what everyone else called "the new normal." This strange new workplace had shifted to where the employees now had equal power. The workers were calling the shots as to whether they went back into the office. They demanded to know what safety protocols were in place. Because of the traumatic experience they had just lived through, they were precise about how they were and were not willing to use their time. In the meantime, employers offered incentives to get employees back to the office in an effort to maintain company culture. Employers were dealing with global supply chain issues, dramatic revenue fluctuations, and suddenly, a disengaged workforce.

Today, leaders are still catching up.

In a 2020 report on employee care, "Workplaces in Crisis: Employee Care Missing the Mark," the Limeade Institute found that 72% of employees were experiencing burnout, compared to 42% before the pandemic. A 2021 *Gallup* article, "US Employee Engagement Needs a Rebound," found that in 2021, employee engagement had dropped to 34% in the US for the first time in a decade.

In 2022, more than four million Americans quit their jobs every month on average. By 2023, over 61% of US workers were considering leaving their jobs and then in 2024, the *Gallup* reports showed that only 30% of employees were engaged in their work. But why?

Your Employees Want More of You as a True Leader

By mid-2023, a swarm of apathy and discontent swept through Corporate America that opened the eyes of many leaders. Employees garnered the strength to demonstrate their dissatisfaction with work primarily via two approaches: Quiet Quitting and "The Great Resignation."

Quiet Quitters essentially did the work required of them and not much more, thereby resisting what had, in some cases, become toxic or exploitative work environments. Following the pandemic, they returned to the workplace after nearly two years of virtual or hybrid work, where they spent designated days in the office and other days working virtually. When they came back full-time, they realized that the place they once spent one-third to nearly one-half of their weekday hours was more of a prison than a paradise. From the perspective of employers, those Quiet Quitters slowly disengaged from their work, doing just enough to get by while still getting paid before they eventually exited or were fired.

During the pandemic, these employees had developed a new way of managing their time and getting work done, free from the office politics and biases that clouded an otherwise peaceful environment. They learned to embrace the freedom of working flexible hours, enjoying time spent with family, and doing leisure activities without the requirement to show up at the office for unnecessary meetings or to satisfy leaders who wanted to see them doing the work. Most often, the quiet quitters were younger employees or those who had less tenure at the workplace.

Those who quit their jobs, ushering in The Great Resignation, were often long-time employees who had devoted years, sometimes decades, of their time, intellect, knowledge, and experience to a company. During the pandemic, these workers got a taste of what retirement might be like. They realized that they could survive financially with less than they thought they'd need. Like the Quiet Quitters, they also came to value the freedom of leisure time. They reassessed their contributions to their companies. They also questioned the company's value of their skills and contributions, leading them to conclude that now, not later, would be the best time to resign or retire to chart a new path for themselves.

All of this left leaders to wonder what they had missed. If employees were this discontented with their work lives, something had been overlooked in the workplace equation. What those leaders learned was that the common denominator was them.

In a 2022 survey of 2,000 American workers conducted by OnePoll on behalf of Bonusly, 46% of employees left a job because they felt unappreciated. Another 65% said they'd work harder if management would notice. Two-thirds reported feeling unappreciated by their employer on a daily basis.

An August 2022 *Harvard Business Review* article titled, "Quitting is About Bad Bosses, Not Bad Employees" found that the least-effective managers have three to four times as many people who fall in the "quiet quitting" category compared to the most-effective leaders. These managers had 14% of their direct reports quietly quitting, and only 20% of those direct reports were willing to give extra effort. But those who were rated the highest at balancing results with relationships saw 62% of their direct reports willing to give extra effort, while only 3% were quietly quitting.

How could so many people come out of the same crisis feeling so differently about the role work plays in their lives and their relationship to their work, employers, and leaders? And what can leaders do about it today? Article after article has advised leaders how to address the Great Resignation and Quiet Quitting, but they're all missing the one ingredient I am certain will begin to solve the problem and heal the relationship between leaders and workers: The one thing your employees can't get anywhere else is you.

At the core of The Great Resignation and Quiet Quitting is bad leadership. You can dress it up however you want, but people resorted to these solutions because they'd had it with the routine of the workplace and their interaction with corporate leaders. Most leaders think they're great leaders, but they're not. Otherwise, why would so many people be leaving their jobs? Surely, there are other reasons people leave a job. Some of those reasons include: toxic work environment (which could include racism, sexism, and "other-isms"), lack of work/life balance, low pay/compensation, unfair treatment, or the need for time flexibility. But at the core of all of these reasons is leadership. You know the saying, "People don't leave bad jobs, they leave bad leaders."

The COVID-19 pandemic and the highly publicized social ills of 2020 revealed a gaping chasm between how leaders thought they were leading and what was really happening. Corporate leaders either got off course or ignored the cries of society regarding diversity, equity, inclusion, and belonging, as well as sexism and racism, the support working parents needed, issues within the LGBTQ+ community, and ability issues.

Even the most effective leaders hadn't quite risen to Ally Leadership level to become the voice and the action-taker for those they lead. Those well-meaning leaders who touted bottom-line, year-over-year growth, and consistent employee satisfaction somehow missed the wellspring of discontent and unrest among their employees. They were so busy doling out the typical annual salary increases and hosting predictable holiday parties that they ignored what people really wanted: leaders who cared more about people than profits; more about equity inside the workplace than equity for shareholders; more about fairness than financials; more about exhibiting empathy, trust, and authenticity than just checking the DEIB box.

Let's face it, employees have wanted more than just a paycheck from their employers since before the pandemic. The labor shortage gave them leverage and the pandemic gave them a new perspective on work. Now, the ball is in your court. You need to see your employees for who they are, and you need to show them who you really are. Because what your employees can't get elsewhere is you. If that sounds scary, I get it. You're not in this leadership thing to make friends; you're in it to make a profit, to secure a legacy, to make an impact on your company and your industry. But as you've learned, leading at an arm's length isn't how true Ally Leadership works. It requires more of you.

Here are a few authentic ways to demonstrate your true self to your employees without losing your edge as a leader:

- Share your personal/professional goals with your team.
- Show enthusiasm for your work and your team's work.
- Ask your team for help on something you're working on.
- Get out from behind your desk and mingle with your team, talk to them about non-work-related topics.
- Be a good listener.
- Be humble.
- Let them know what you are learning or reading.
- Think about creative ways to celebrate your team's accomplishments.

Although leaders missed the signals that we were drifting off course, there is a way to find our way back, to course-correct, and to chart a new, better path altogether. It's possible. Just ask a pilot.

Stay on Course: The 1 in 60 Rule

In aviation, there is a rule called the 1 in 60 Rule. This is a navigational formula that is used by all pilots to get back on course. If a pilot flies off course by just 1 degree, by the time they fly 60 miles, they will be 1 mile off course. And it continues to multiply. One degree off course from L.A. to New York has a plane missing LaGuardia by 40 miles. Obviously, this can be extremely dangerous. That is why the best pilots constantly monitor that they are still on course and adjust accordingly.

The airlines are a massive logistical puzzle. Flying off course is not only a safety issue, but it also impacts the Federal Aviation Administration's air space and their air traffic controller process and procedures. It impacts passengers and their arrival and departure times, airports and their gate availability, airlines and their fuel cost and consumption, and some airports (particularly those near neighborhoods) have noise restrictions meaning airplanes can only fly in and out of the airport during certain times so as not to impact the residents. A lot relies on a pilot, the leader of the aircraft, to consistently monitor that they are always on course.

As an Ally Leader, you have so many demands throughout the course of a day that it's easy to get off course. Just like a good pilot, there are actions you can take to get back on course. Consider this the 1 in 60 Rule for Ally Leadership:

1. Establish the Error: Pay attention to your attention.
2. Establish the Correction.
3. Get Back on Course.

Before you get excited and think, "Wow, that sounds pretty easy!" remember that all of the steps are taking place while the plane is still flying over 500 miles per hour, or while you are still managing projects and leading people. In other words, things are still moving. Nothing has stopped or slowed down to allow time to reset. The weather (social events) is still a factor, air traffic congestion (busy days) is still happening, ground holds (delays) are still a possibility, the tower (meetings and delays with customer, clients, and shareholders) may have you circling, all while the crew (employees, coworkers, and colleagues) are still trying to do the work necessary to get back on course.

In business, you implement your Ally Leadership 1 in 60 Rules in the same way: meetings are still taking place, fires still need to be put out, your board is still requesting items, company results still need to be achieved, company culture still needs to be developed, employee engagement still needs attention, and crises still need to be averted. Just like a pilot, you cannot wait until things settle down in order to get back on course. In business, things never stop. Velocity, both good and bad, are still happening. Becoming an Ally Leader is not something you can set aside time to do later. There will never be a convenient time to get started. Now is the time.

Just like a pilot, you need some navigation aids, or "navaids," to help you stay on course, even in strong crosswinds.

Navaid #1: Establish the Error: Pay attention to your attention

If you have a workforce that is "quietly quitting" or simply not as engaged or as productive as you would like, don't get discouraged. You can fix this by paying attention to your attention, meaning, be conscious to what you notice in the workplace. Instead of doing the same things with the same people and departments, you have to expand your attention and be aware of the people and the environment as a whole. Remember, what they want is you and they want you to pay attention.

Be an ALLY. Talk to them, ask them questions about them, listen to them, learn from them, and give them you by sharing some of your own story. This is how you will see them for who they are, not who you think they are.

Back in 2020, after my husband Sam suffered a stroke, he had to go through speech and physical rehabilitation for several months so he could learn to walk, talk, and write again. It was a tough time for him and for our family. He had always been independent, and suddenly, it was like starting over.

He had to retune his attention. Attention simply means to "give special care." There are four levels of attention all humans exhibit: selective, sustained, divided, and alternating.

1. **Selective attention** is when you pay attention to a specific thing, even though there's competing stimuli. Perhaps an employee is telling you about a problem and you're focused on them and not the noise in the office, your phone buzzing in your pocket, or lunch being delivered to someone else's desk.

2. **Sustained attention** is what you're doing now. You are giving attention to this book for a sustained amount of time.

3. **Divided attention** is what we would call multitasking. Like checking your texts on your phone while listening to the speaker in a meeting. We all think we can divide our attention that way, but we really can't listen and comprehend well when we multitask.

4. **Alternating attention** is shifting your focus from one task to another. Students do this when learning something new and practicing the function of the new information. You read instructions while carrying out the function you are learning, much like in a hands-on training course. This is the attention you will exhibit as you learn Ally Leadership techniques and practice them daily.

Navaid #2: Establish the Correction

You are not the leader you were years ago because you have evolved. Now, more than ever, leaders must evolve. One of the ways to do that is to focus on courageous human connection, what we've long called "soft skills." Too often, soft skills get treated like warm, fuzzy niceties, something to give lip service to after we're done with the P&L statements, the stockholder meetings, and quarterly projections.

Consider the statistics about Quiet Quitting and The Great Resignation. Employees are not leaving because of spreadsheets. They're leaving because there is not enough of a connection to stay. To course correct requires you to boost your courage. Be vulnerable, get present, and master the art of asking, listening, learning, and taking action. Winston Churchill said, "Courage is what it takes to stand up and speak. Courage is also what it takes to sit down and listen."

You might think you understand everything there is to know about connection, because you were born to connect. Without connection, our species would have died out generations ago because we couldn't have survived the elements and the saber-toothed tigers on our own. But today, you are not connecting with your employees. If you were, there would be no Great Resignation.

One way to connect better is to shift from extrinsic motivation to intrinsic motivation. Extrinsic motivation is driven by external rewards, like playing with your child to prevent a tantrum. Intrinsic motivation comes from within, so playing with your child to feel connected. At work, extrinsic motivations tend to be financial, such as paychecks and raises. Intrinsic motivations look like working hard because you feel energized by the positive work environment.

Leaders tend to fling extrinsic solutions at intrinsic issues, like handing out branded lunchboxes to encourage employees to return to the office. In my office, we did the usual extrinsic potluck luncheon at Thanksgiving-time, but I also met one-on-one with each of my direct reports to tell them, in great detail, why I was thankful for them. They weren't allowed to say anything until I was finished, and boy, were those meetings powerful and special.

So, now that you've established the correction, what's next?

Navaid #3: Get Back on Course

Most leaders will give their employees reviews during review time and not a minute before. But the best managers for these times keep an open conversation with their teams throughout the year about their needs and about their futures.

You want to be the leader who everyone flocks to. You may be under the illusion that being that kind of leader happens by simply offering more pay, but that's the easy way out. Employees want more than just the paycheck for services rendered. They also want your time, your attention, your mentorship, your constructive criticism, and your support. They want you. And that's the thing they can't get anywhere else. Even if you've missed the mark as an Ally Leader in the past—like my friend Ted did with the group call that became more about him than his team—you can apply this Navaid to get back on track.

Ally Leadership and getting or staying on course happens minute by minute, hour by hour, and day by day. It's already part of you. Like a pilot, you have a lot of souls onboard your proverbial aircraft, and they trust you to get this right. Authenticity, caring for others, and striving to win all come naturally for you as a human being.

Practice the techniques in this book to continue to win.

- Take the Ally Leadership Assessment at stephaniechung.com/bonus.
- Acknowledge your mental comfort zone of familiarity.
- Notice and remove the "other-isms" within your mental space and workplace.
- Learn what true Ally Leadership is, how to do it, and embrace what's in it for you.
- Acknowledge your areas of privilege.
- Consistently practice authentic, not performative, Ally Leadership.
- Review your company's DEIB policies and improve them regularly.
- Check your bias often.

- Review your course and correct accordingly.

- Give employees what they really want: You.

By implementing the 1 in 60 Rule, you can make the required constant adjustments to your leadership to improve the company's culture, attract and retain top talent, and accelerate productivity. Use the philosophy of the 1 in 60 Rule to get back on track to your natural instincts of trust and empathy for Ally Leadership.

Author Adam Grant once said, "Passion often *follows* effort, versus driving it." What he went on to say is that no one likes failing all the time. Just because you fail at something at first doesn't mean you're not good at it. Often, you will become passionate about something the better you get at it. The same is true for Ally Leadership.

Exercising your Ally Leadership muscle might sometimes cause muscle fatigue, but stay with it because you are hardwired for this. Per Grant, many people feel like they have to master a knowledge or skill before they can use it. That is incorrect. Research shows that the best way to use your knowledge is while you are acquiring it. As you move forward along your Ally Leadership journey, keep this in mind. Don't stall your efforts simply because you haven't yet mastered it. Instead, step out and begin using these new skills so you can eventually master them. Ultimately, the more mistakes you make, the more knowledge and understanding you gain in any subject.

The two most common mistakes of leaders who practice Ally Leadership are:

1. Falling back into old habits because "things got busy" or you got tired. So, instead of asking, listening, and learning you decide to speed things up and just assume.

2. Getting too comfortable. Once you've gotten a few wins under your belt, it's not uncommon to think you now know best. So, you stop asking, listening, and learning, but you do take action. Unfortunately, your action misses the mark because you do what makes sense to you from your viewpoint, which may not properly align with your colleagues who are not like you or don't have your lived experiences.

When mistakes happen, as they often do, don't be discouraged. Hopefully, you've created an environment where everyone feels seen, appreciated, and psychologically safe enough to point out the error. Thank them for the feedback, make the proper adjustments by getting back on course, and then press forward in a better stance.

Switching from the scramble-to-fix-it leadership skills to lead a forever-changed workplace where everyone feels valued and where Ally Leaders are the heroes, not the villains, is bound to improve your company's culture and your leadership clout. It will also help you attract and retain top talent and ultimately improve productivity.

When employees are engaged, they become productive, and they are drawn to you. When you become the Ally Leader everyone wants, your team is productive and they don't leave. The company thrives, customers are satisfied, and the bottom line grows. Essentially, everyone wins! And when others win, you win. That is the goal of Ally Leadership.

GROWING UP ON ACTIVE MILITARY bases, I knew early on what I wanted to do as a career. My dad was a Master Sergeant in the US Air Force, so I grew up around planes, hearing them take off and land. Even as a little girl, I knew I wanted to be in aviation. But I didn't know what I could do. Whenever I would see pictures of aviators, I would see men as pilots and women as flight attendants. And none of those pictures ever looked like me, a black girl. So, I didn't know exactly what I could do in aviation, but I knew it was my calling.

My very first job was loading luggage at Boston's Logan Airport. To make extra money, I would go upstairs to work at the ticket counter and check people in for their flights. While there, I would see our airline's VP of Sales, Jim, come and go. Jim was a short white guy with silvery grey hair and a thick southern accent.

One day, he pulled me aside and said, "Stephanie, every time I come through this city, I see you at the ticket counter, smiling and serving customers. I think you should be in sales."

Okay?

Because Jim had noticed me working at the ticket counter always with a smile, he trusted that I could do the job of sales. I can't know what assumptions Jim might have had about me prior to that day, but in that moment he had gotten over them. I had done the same thing about him, too. I stopped assuming what I'd learned growing up in the 1960s, specifically that Jim was a good ol' Southern boy with no use for the likes of me. Thankfully, Jim shattered that notion that I had adopted from sheer observation and the conversations overheard among some of the adults in my life. I didn't know it then, but that invitation from Jim propelled me into the life I knew I was destined for.

Twenty-nine years after that fateful day, I rose up through the ranks to become the first black person in US history to run a major private aviation company. I became the leader I am today because Jim was the kind of leader he was. He believed in someone—namely me—and took a chance, a risk that I could do what he expected of me. He assumed I would use the skills I demonstrated and rise to meet the demands of a new position. More importantly, Jim did three key things: 1) He paid attention and looked past his assumptions to see me for who I was; 2) He courageously connected at a time in history when doing so wasn't expected; and 3) He shifted me on course towards an opportunity he believed I could handle and one I hadn't even considered for myself. Jim was an Ally Leader.

Jim couldn't have known that his simple act of noticing me, acknowledging my work ethic, and moving me into an ideal position would impact my life and career in the way it did. Equally as important, Jim's simple act of Ally Leadership not only impacted my life but also altered history and now allows me to impact other lives as well through my keynote speeches, my books, and my participation on influential boards that make an impact in the world.

Like Jim, you have innumerable opportunities to make a positive impact on your coworkers. You can be an average leader who gets it done or you can be an above-average leader who not only gets it done but also leaves a legacy while doing so.

What holds you back from paying attention, connecting, and taking the actions to become an Ally Leader? Imagine what would happen if you became the leader everyone wants to work for. How would that impact your career, your company, your life?

I've been blessed to have worked with so many people who were not like me. This was both exhilarating and exhausting because people, all people, can sometimes be incredibly complex, extraordinarily kind, and downright messy—but hey, isn't that a perfect definition of life itself.

No two people are the same. We look different, we think different, we talk different, we are different, and yet we've all been placed here on earth together. Why didn't God just make us all the same; it would have been much easier, right? There would be no disagreements, no wars, no hate, no one to challenge our thought process, no one would think they're better than anyone else. All of our lives would be easier—boring, but easier for sure.

Is it possible that God saw something that we have yet to see? Perhaps there's power and purpose in our differences?

If you believe, like I do, that God doesn't make mistakes, then he had a reason why he chose to make us all different. What those reasons are, I don't know, but I imagine that he's counting on us to get together and get it together so we can use our collective power and purpose for good.

The type of good that brings meaning to life, the type of good that allows us to answer the age-old question, "Why am I here?"

As I began to embrace people who were not like me, a funny thing happened: my purpose in life became clearer. Clear because I opened myself up to learn from those individuals; this allowed me to become better. A better leader, friend, mother, wife, an overall better person.

My hope is that this book will help you be a better leader, friend, and overall better person because you'll have a new appreciation for those who are not like you.

ABOUT THE AUTHOR

STEPHANIE CHUNG IS NOT JUST an author; she's a force of strategic innovation, a beacon of change, and a titan in the world of business growth and human capital management. With more than thirty years of experience, Stephanie has cultivated a reputation for turning challenges into opportunities, and transforming growing businesses into thriving hubs of success.

As a former Chief Growth Officer for Wheels Up, Stephanie spearheaded a growth strategy that not only elevated revenues but also fostered market expansion, resulting in a significant increase in diverse membership. Prior to her tenure at Wheels Up, Stephanie blazed trails as the first African American to helm a private jet company, JetSuite. Under her visionary leadership, JetSuite evolved from a mere service provider to a symbol of luxury and excellence, garnering accolades such as being named one of the Best Places To Work by the Human Rights Campaign and *Dallas Business Journal's* 100 Fastest Growing Private Companies. Stephanie's illustrious career also includes pivotal roles at American Airlines, Flexjet, and Bombardier Aerospace, where she engineered revenue generation strategies that achieved remarkable success.

Stephanie's impact extends far beyond the boardroom—beyond her professional achievements, she is a dedicated advocate, serving on the Make-A-Wish Board and the Advisory Council for the National Business Aviation Association. She is a member of Business Executives for National Security (BENS), collaborating with senior national security leaders to address complex challenges facing the nation. These achievements and more have earned her recognition as one of *Adweek's* "Women Trailblazers", *Ebony's* Power 100, and *Robb Report's* "23 Black Visionaries Who are Changing the Luxury World." She has appeared on ABC, CNBC, CBS, and other national TV outlets and has been celebrated in publications such as *Forbes, Barron's, Worth, Essence,* and *D CEO Magazine.* Her insights have also graced the pages of *Inc.* and *Black Enterprise Magazine.*

A captivating keynote speaker, Stephanie's influence transcends borders. Her work has been translated into sixty languages. Her journey is a testament to the power of strategic thinking, resilience, and unwavering dedication to excellence.

ACKNOWLEDGMENTS

THANK YOU TO EVERYONE I'VE ever worked with, served beside, or led. You have taught me so much. This book is a compilation of our time together, the "heck ya" moments and the "oh geez" moments! The names in the stories have been changed to protect your privacy but the raw emotions of it all—they're real.

I'd like to give a special shoutout to my tribe who supported me throughout my book journey. First, I'd like to give a special shoutout to my bestie John Rood. John, you were there from the beginning, from when this book was a wild thought in my head to its inception. I thank you for your sound advice, your steadfast support, your ability to challenge my thinking, and for sharing your unique experiences with leading people who are not like you. The world is a better place because you're in it. Thank you for being a true friend.

A special shoutout goes to two of my favorite pastors, David Ashcraft and Craig Groeschel. You've both been so supportive and have given me great guidance on how to address the uncomfortable stuff, the things that aren't talked about but need to be said. I so appreciate your heart and your wisdom.

Thomas Fry gets a huge thank you. Can you believe how far we've come, TFry? Many years ago, you had the foresight to see this long before I could see this for myself. Thank you for pushing me when I didn't want to be pushed out into the forefront. You, my friend, are the original "OG" when it comes to the Stephanie Chung brand.

Thanks to my friends at Washington Speakers Bureau who encouraged me to write the book in the first place. My amazing publishing team (Melanie, Jenn, and Nicole) at Elite Publishing, my copy editor Karin Crompton, and the world's best book coach, Anita Henderson of Write Your Life. I'd also like to thank my Ally Leadership Assessment Advisor, Neurologist, Dr Philippe Douyon.

To my rockstar beta readers, you are awesome! Thank you Wilma Sumrell, Brittany Chung, John Rood, David Ashcraft, Andrea Lee, Lisa Stone, Kim Evans, Beth Garvey, Bill Dolney, Sean Lee, Zach Suchin, Kenneth Palacios, and Holly Sheridan. I'd also like to thank my Foreword writers, John Rood (mentioned above) and the Chief Trouble Maker Shelley Zalis.

Shelley, you and I often joke about being the black & white version of each other. I love your commitment, tenacity, and dogmatic approach to women's equality. I am excited to partner with you to help close the gender pay gap once and for all!

To Vanessa Van Edwards, you have been a blessing in so many ways. Thank you for always being so generous with your time, insight, and connections. I value our friendship and I value you. Thank you, Michael Amalfitano, for our impromptu brainstorming session on the intersectionality of athletes, soldiers, and Ally Leaders. Your comments were most helpful.

I want to give a special shoutout to all the folks at Brand Knew. My Peeps! In the words of Tina Turner, you're "simply the best"!! Thank you for your professionalism, thank you for making me laugh out loud each week, and thank you for everything you do to help further my reach. I couldn't do this without you.

Lastly, I'd like to thank everyone who purchased this book because it shows that you want to be part of the Ally Leadership Movement. You want to do your part to help make this world a better place, not by trying to force people to be more like you, but instead by getting excited because they're not like you. Let's all go out there and win together!

Made in the USA
Columbia, SC
22 April 2025

57015680R00093